PCC
ACCOUNTABILITY

The Charities Act 2011
and the PCC

5th edition

Guidance on accounts, reports and scrutiny including
the Church Accounting Regulations 2006 prescribed
by the Business Committee of the General Synod

The Charities Act and the PCC

Church House
Great Smith Street
London
SW1P 3AZ

ISBN 978-0-7151-1112-3

First published 2006 by
Church House Publishing.

Fifth edition published in 2017
for the House of Bishops of the
General Synod of the Church
of England

Copyright © The Archbishops'
Council 2006, 2017

Typeset by ForDesign
Printed and bound by
CPI Group (UK) Ltd.,
Croydon CR0 4YY

Contents

chapter 1

Introduction and Legal Overview

1.1 Background

This publication has been designed to provide all users with a comprehensive and up-to-date reference guide to assist in the preparation of the requisite PCC Annual Report and accounts.

Introduction to Charity Accounting

Charities have a major impact on our society, funding or supporting community work that otherwise, if it would seem to be outside the total responsibility of government, would not happen! So it is easy to see why governments are interested in all charities. They want to ensure that money given to charities is spent on the charity's aims and not wasted, so that people will keep giving.

To achieve this aim successive UK governments have been developing charity law for more than 400 years. They have made charity trustees more and more responsible for the work and finances of the charity. The members of the PCC are charity trustees. The Charities Act (2011) defines charities as organisations that aim to provide 'public benefit' in one or more charitable areas or 'purposes'. It has also reinforced the Charity Commission's legal powers to be able to support and regulate charities.

The Charity Commission created the Charities SORP ('Accounting and Reporting by Charities: Statement of Recommended Practice'), to give us clear guidelines on what information to keep and what reports to produce to meet our legal obligations. The Church of England has adopted the SORP as its standard basis for annual financial reporting by parishes, so that now we can provide the same information to both the government (for the general public) and the wider Church.

What does this mean for you as a parish?

As PCC members we are the charity trustees of the parish. We therefore need to understand what money is coming into the church, how we are spending it and why. In order to give a clear account of how the money has been received and spent, each parish has to produce the reports required by law.

These accounts and reports help us to tell people how their money supports the mission of the church. They will also help us to show that the money given to us for running the parish or for specific aims such as youth or building work was used for those purposes. As PCC members we are responsible for the money, how it is looked after and for providing clear information about all of the money that belongs to the church.

The first step in providing the correct reports is to decide which kind of annual accounts you need to produce and how these will be externally examined. There are two alternative ways of preparing annual accounts: either the Receipts and Payments basis or the Accruals basis.

The reader can select the relevant chapters depending on whether they are producing accounts on a Receipts and Payments basis or are adopting accruals accounting. The following flow chart is the starting point and should be used to determine which method should be adopted. Chapters 5 to 8 provide detailed guidance and examples for each method, while Chapter 9 includes guidance on moving from one accounting to another.

This revision of the guide has been produced by sub-groups of the Diocesan Accounts Group. The sub-groups comprise representation from diocesan and national church staff and external professional advisers. The members of the sub-groups are acknowledged at the back of this guide.

The content of this book is accessible online on the Church of England's Parish Resources website at: www.parishresources.org.uk.

Further guidance can be found on the Charity Commission website at: www.charity-commission.gov.uk. Another useful source of guidance is the Association of Church Accountants and Treasurers (ACAT). This is a national charity that provides resources to support the work of treasurers in churches of all Christian denominations. ACAT provides a programme of training events including foundation courses for new treasurers and more detailed workshops on specific topics that are relevant to PCC governance and financial administration. Further information is available on ACAT's website: www.acat.uk.com.

1.2 Regime of public accountability

There are two different bases for the preparation of annual financial statements, depending on the size of the PCC in terms of gross annual income. There are also two different forms of external scrutiny of the financial statements.

The requirements and options are summarised on the following flow chart.

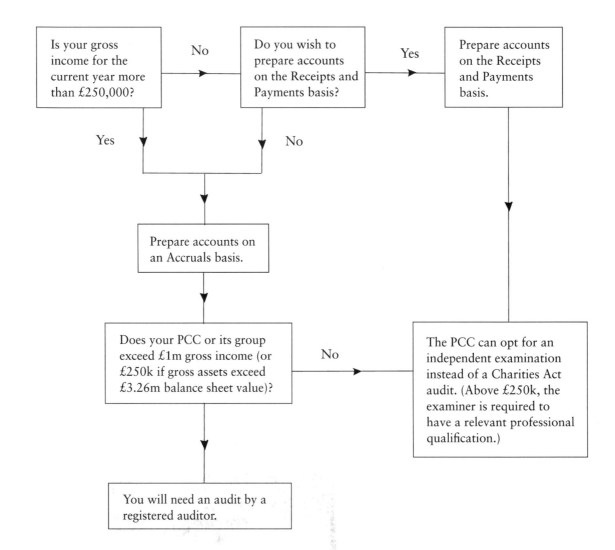

1.3   Making the choice

This section describes whether accounts on the Receipts and Payments or Accruals accounting basis must or may be prepared.

In order to discover which aspects of the Regulations apply to the PCC, its statutory 'gross income' must first be calculated according to the Charity Commission's rules. The PCC can then identify where it stands in the accounting framework for charity accounts.

The Charity Commission's rules for calculating gross income allow you to do this by reference to cash receipts as long as the figure of £250,000 is not exceeded on that basis. If it is exceeded you will have to prepare accounts on the Accruals basis, even if this would result in showing a gross income figure of less than £250,000 in the Statement of Financial Activities (SOFA).

If the PCC's income for the year exceeds £500,000, the PCC is deemed to be a 'larger charity'. There are then extra disclosure requirements for the Annual Report and the accounts and a cash flow statement is mandatory under FRS 102.

How do you decide? The basic rule is to calculate the gross income of your parish (that is all monies received as income before any payments have been made out of them or any costs deducted, and excluding any trust capital monies received for endowment or any loan monies). If the total is:

● Up to £250,000 for the year, you can choose to prepare either Accruals accounts or the Receipts and Payments-based accounts.

● Over £250,000 a year, you must prepare Accruals accounts.

If your income is up to £250,000 per year, Receipts and Payments is the easier form of annual accounting for your parish. Unless there are particular reasons why accruals accounts are needed for your parish, new treasurers are advised to choose Receipts and Payments.

Accruals accounts are required by law if the PCC's annual gross income is over £250,000.

1.4   What is the gross income of the PCC for the purposes of Receipts and Payments accounting?

The gross income is the total amount of money recorded as income of the PCC in all unrestricted and restricted funds but not amounts of money received as capital (endowment funds), nor the proceeds of disposal of any assets held for investment use or for the PCC's own continuing use. Gross income receipts should be recorded before the deduction of any costs or expenses and includes the following:

● Money received as voluntary income;

● Money received from activities for generating funds (fundraising for church activities);

● Investment income receipts;

● Receipts from fees and charges for charitable activities;

● Any amounts of money taken out of endowment capital as income during the year (i.e. transferred into income funds or otherwise spent as income).

The following items should be excluded:

● a loan received by the PCC;

● the repayment to the PCC of a loan made by them;

● the proceeds of the sale of investments or 'functional fixed assets' (such as a hall, which is held for the purpose of furthering the mission of the church) or any gain or profit on their sale;

● donations grant or legacies received in money by the PCC as endowment capital.

The table below summarises the gross income of the PCC on the Receipts and Payments basis.

Include		Exclude
Voluntary income receipts		
	• All non-endowment donations of money from individuals • Grants from organisations • Monetary bequests other than endowments • Loans written off by lenders	• Grants received as an advance but repayable if certain criteria are not met, i.e. to be treated as loans • Grants promised but not yet received • Donations received as capital (endowment) funds where only the income can be used by the PCC • Loans received by the PCC • Repayment to the PCC of a loan made by them
Cash received for activities for generating funds		
	• Gross income monies before the deduction of any costs or expenses incurred	• Associated expenses that are very small (not material) and where it is impractical to identify them separately
Investment income receipts		
	• Interest on deposit accounts • Dividends paid both in cash but not in kind, e.g. shares • Investment income derived from endowment funds	• Proceeds of the sale of investments or 'functional fixed assets', e.g. a hall or curate's house held for the purpose of furthering the mission of the church
Income receipts from charitable activities		
	• Gross income before the deduction of any costs or expenses, e.g. heating	• Amounts received on behalf of other parties, e.g. verger, organist, choir that are to be paid straight out again • Fees collected on behalf of the clergy and diocese

Where a PCC holds endowment funds, the following items must be included in the gross income calculation:

- any permanent or expendable endowment spent, borrowed or spent as income and therefore transferred to income funds during the year;

- any permanent endowment 'unapplied total return' allocated or transferred to income funds during the year.

Further detail of the various items of income is given in Chapter 2.

Points to note

- In calculating the gross income, there should be no netting off of expenditure and income (no cancelling income against expenditure). Suppose the parish runs a fete and raises £1,000 after charging £500 for expenses. They should show £1,500 of income and £500 of expenditure. If the netting off is small and it is impracticable to identify the precise amount, then this requirement to 'gross' up can be ignored.

- If in doubt, include an item rather than leave it out – unless that takes the PCC into costlier regulatory regime (e.g. statutory audit) when professional advice will be needed. The rules are to help people to understand the financial statements more easily and to help PCCs have the information they need for managing their affairs properly. These aims should be kept in mind when deciding which small items should be included or excluded, either gross or net.

- Money may be received to build a new building or to improve an existing building. If the funds raised create an endowment (due to the capital nature of the project for which the donor intended the gift to be used, i.e. to equip the PCC with assets for longer-term use), or the asset to be improved is an endowment asset, the funds raised are endowment and should be excluded from the calculation of gross income.

- If there is a major appeal for activities or repair or a major non-endowed legacy is received in a year it will be quite possible for the gross income in that year to increase from, say, £100,000 to over £250,000. If this happens, no attempt must be made to manipulate the figures by artificially accelerating or delaying activities. As the PCC will be handling larger sums of money it is only right that it should have to account for them in a more rigorous way.

- The law requires all gross income to be included (e.g. any occasional non-endowed legacies and grants), even if its inclusion makes the financial size of the parish much bigger than was previously the case and than the PCC expects. The calculations are made to arrive at a figure of genuine gross income.

Legal overview

This section provides an overview of the requirements of the Charities Act 2011 and associated regulations and relates them to both large and small Parochial Church Councils.

1.5 The duties of the PCC

The members of the PCC are the charity trustees and are the 'persons having the general control and management of the administration of the charity' (Charities Act 2011, s177).

The trustees are entrusted with the PCC's funds. They must:

- Always act responsibly;

- Ensure that all decisions are taken for the benefit of the PCC;

- Always act in accordance with the governing documents, principally the PCC (Powers) Measure 1956 as amended by the Ecclesiastical Property Measure 2015;

- Not seek personal benefit (commitment to the cause must be the main reason for serving as a trustee).

The PCC is responsible for all parish finance, its management and control, including the appointment of a treasurer. While it may delegate some of its duties, for example, to District Church Councils (DCCs), this does not remove its legal responsibilities. These include:

- Keeping 'proper accounting records', which include the annual financial statements, and which must be preserved for at least six years from the end of the financial year to which they relate. The records must be sufficient to:

    - show and explain all the PCC's transactions;

    - disclose the PCC's financial position at any time with reasonable accuracy;

    - enable the required statutory accounts to be prepared;

    - show on a day-to-day basis all Receipts and Payments and what they were for;

    - record all assets and liabilities.

- Ensuring that the finances of the PCC are under its control and decision making is only delegated if the PCC can ensure that its wishes will be followed.

- Arranging for a suitable independent examination or audit of the financial statements.

- Preparing the Annual Report and accounts (financial statements), which must be presented to the Annual Parochial Church Meeting in accordance with the requirements of the Church Representation Rules.

1.6   Accounting framework

The accounting, auditing and reporting regime for Church of England PCCs is contained in the following documentation:

- *Charities Act 2011*

- *Charities (Accounts and Reports) Regulations 2008*

- *Statement of Recommended Practice on Accounting and Reporting by Charities SORP (FRS 102)*

In addition, financial statements for PCCs must be prepared in accordance with the following:

- *The PCCs (Powers) Measure 1956*

- *The Church Representation Rules (CRRs)*

- *The Church Accounting Regulations 2006*, which form the link between the CRRs and the requirements of the Charities Act.

The law makes it clear that charities are accountable to the public for the resources they control. Charities receive funds for public benefit and must demonstrate to the public that they have observed the trust placed in them in the handling and use of those funds.

Under the Charities Act 2011, all PCCs below the special registration threshold (currently £100,000 per annum) are excepted charities and do not have to file annual returns or Annual Reports and accounts with the Charity Commission. Details of the registration process for PCCs over this threshold are available on the Parishes Resources website (www.parishresources.org).

All PCCs must prepare their Annual Report and financial statements in accordance with the Charities Act 2011 and the regulations and, as with any other charity, must make them available to the public.

1.7   Accounting for the legal entity

The general principle is that statutory accounts must be produced for the legal entity.

That means that PCCs (as the legal entity) must prepare appropriate Annual Reports and accounts that are in accordance with the Charities Act and the Charities (Accounts and Reports) Regulations, as applicable, and this responsibility cannot be delegated to others.

This is quite straightforward in most cases but questions arise when considering teams, united benefices and pluralities.

1.8   United benefices and pluralities

The legal entity is the PCC and not the united benefice, team or plurality, and it is the PCC that must produce accounts in the statutory format.

The thresholds are tested for each PCC, which must each appoint an independent examiner or, if appropriate, an auditor. Providing the independence test holds good, the same person may agree to serve more than one PCC.

1.9 Teams

Teams vary a great deal and the guidance on how to meet the requirements of the Charities Act varies with the circumstances. For example:

- Teams that comprise a number of separate PCCs must produce separate accounts that meet the statutory requirements at the level of each PCC. Of course, a summary financial statement can be produced at the level of the team, but there is no requirement to do so and there are no constraints on the format.

- Other teams may have been formed on the basis of a single parish comprising one PCC with more than one place of worship but without DCCs. As before, accounts that meet the statutory requirements must be produced for the PCC. Of course, there is nothing to stop the production of non-statutory financial statements that in each case relate to one of the different congregations with its place of worship, but there is no requirement to do so and there are no constraints on the format. It may be appropriate for such information to take the form of notes to the PCC accounts (so that they are part of that body of statutory information).

1.10 District Church Councils (DCCs)

A situation may arise where pastoral reorganisation has combined separate parishes into a new single parish and thus a single PCC with DCCs as its 'branches' to retain the sense of local community.

In both these cases statutory accounts must be produced at the level of the PCC, though these can of course be based on the aggregation of 'branch' accounts that may be produced by the DCCs for their own congregations.

While certain internal management responsibilities can be passed down from the PCC to its DCCs, this does not amount to delegated legal and financial responsibility, which must by law stay with the PCC as the only body with legal standing. DCCs cannot have assets of their own, they do not have body corporate status like the PCC, nor are they legally distinct from it, and so they should not be taking financial decisions and signing contracts, for which they lack the requisite legal standing. Of course, the PCC can decide to leave DCCs free to operate within an agreed budget, but the PCC is the only legal entity that is able to enter into a contract or institute legal proceedings.

Where DCCs have been preparing their own accounts there is no reason why this should not continue, but these are then only 'branch' accounts, to be brought together at the PCC level to form the latter's statutory accounts, and therefore careful co-ordination between the DCCs and the PCC over the final examination/audit of the PCC's statutory accounts will be needed.

1.11 Aggregation of PCC and DCC accounts

If the DCCs have been used to preparing and publishing their own, separate accounts, the need to aggregate the accounts at PCC level may be a cause for concern to them. Consideration of the following may mitigate the circumstances for them:

- If the DCCs are very small and the PCC of which they form a part is below the accruals accounts threshold, the statutory requirements should be relatively easily met by taking the Receipts and Payments accounts for the individual DCCs and preparing a combined statement of receipts and payments to go with the PCC's statement of all assets and liabilities. An Annual Report will be required at PCC level which could have general details for the PCC and short reports on activities from each DCC.

- If the aggregated gross income exceeds £250,000 per annum, then the statutory requirement is for a single statement of accounts on the accruals basis covering all the DCCs and other transactions at PCC level. It should be noted that if either the gross assets threshold of £3.26m is exceeded at this level of income or else (regardless of balance sheet considerations) the income threshold of £1m (£500,000, per annum prior to 2015) is exceeded, then the accounts must be audited. The group accounting threshold is also £1m.

- The independent examiner's task may appear onerous but the person responsible for the examination does not have to carry it all out themselves. The PCC will need to appoint an independent examiner (who will need to meet the requirements of the task) but the examiner might choose to delegate aspects of the work to others, particularly if a number of congregations have to be covered. In this way each DCC may have its part of the aggregated accounts examined by a different person, but the DCC examiners would all be working to the PCC's statutory examiner, who will take sole legal responsibility for any work they have been delegated to carry out. It is the PCC examiner who is responsible for agreeing the programme of work of the local examiners, reviewing the results of their work and then reporting in statutory terms on the statutory accounts of the PCC.

It cannot be avoided that aggregation at PCC level may increase the gross income of the PCC to a level that means that it crosses a threshold and enters a more rigorous regime.

It should be noted that a PCC with DCCs does not require a common bank account. The PCC may arrange for each DCC to have its own bank account but this will need to be subject to the overall control of the PCC and subject to an assessment of any risks and benefits of operating multiple bank accounts.

Joint arrangements

Some groups of PCCs operate a group or PCC account, to which PCCs contribute. It is used to fund joint activities, such as the incumbent's working expenses or a magazine. This fund may be accounted for in one of two ways:

- One PCC in the group may control the fund as a restricted fund and receive grants from the other PCCs in the group. This PCC then accounts for the fund and the other PCCs show their contribution as a grant. If the fund is a significant sum of money, the PCC may not wish to adopt this method as it may move them into a more complex accounting regime.

- The joint account may be handled as an informal 'joint venture' (called a 'joint arrangement' in the SORP), where each PCC accounts for its share of the total fund. A PCC treasurer may operate an account, which serves the joint activity. The expenditure on the account should be allocated appropriately to each PCC. The PCC treasurer running the account should not treat payments received from the other PCCs as income. Any assets or liabilities generated within the account also need to be allocated to each contributing PCC at the year end.

1.12 Local ecumenical partnerships (LEPs)

Where a parish is part of a Local Ecumenical Partnership (LEP), the Annual Report and accounts must be prepared in accordance with the constitution for the LEP. Some denominations have a year-end date other than 31 December and the constitution will establish the relevant accounting date for the particular LEP. The constitutions may establish different legal rights and obligations for the participating denominations and the accounting consequences will need to be determined on a case-by-case basis.

1.13 Registration with the Charity Commission or excepted status

The Charities Act 2011 specifies that PCCs and other excepted charities with gross income in excess of a special registration threshold (currently £100,000 per annum) must register with the Charity Commission.

Dispensation from registration can be sought from the Charity Commission where the income threshold of £100,000 per annum has been exceeded only because of an exceptional and non-recurring item.

Details of the registration process are available on the Parish Resources website (www.parishresources.org).

Registered charities must:

- disclose their registration status on all relevant documents, e.g. letterheads, website, cheques, invoices and receipts (e.g. a registered charity or Charity No. xxxxxxx);

- submit an annual return to the Charity Commission;

- submit a copy of the annual report and accounts to the Charity Commission (unless PCC income has fallen below £25,000 for the year).

Excepted status remains for all PCCs that are not registered with the Charity Commission.

Excepted charities do not have a charity registration number and do not have to file an Annual Report and accounts with the Commission unless specifically requested.

All PCCs, registered and excepted, must, however (under the Church Representation Rules) send a copy of the annual report and accounts to the Secretary of the Diocesan Board of Finance, within 28 days of the PCC's Annual Parochial Church Meeting. They must also be provided to the public upon written request (a fee may be charged). PCCs are charitable bodies and may, inter alia, claim tax refunds on Gift Aid contributions, receive investment income without deduction of income tax and in general enjoy all the other tax reliefs available to registered charities.

1.14 Basic overview of PCC accounts

In preparing their accounts PCCs must:

- account for their incoming resources and the investment or expenditure of their resources in at least three main categories: unrestricted funds, restricted funds and endowment funds;

- aggregate the accounts of any other parts of the organisation that the PCC controls;

- account for their stewardship of those resources:

    - either in cash-based accounts, consisting of Receipts and Payments account(s) with a Statement of Assets and Liabilities, distinguishing any endowed or other funds restricted under trust law;

    - or in accruals accounts, which show a true and fair view, consisting of a SOFA, a balance sheet and notes to give certain additional information;

- identify and, if accruals accounts are prepared, put a proper value on their assets, to help the public understand the PCC's financial position;

- report on their finances and activities in such a way that the general public can understand what has been going on;

- have the accounts scrutinised by an independent examiner if they are not required to be audited by a registered auditor, under the Charities Act and the Church Accounting Regulations.

1.15 Good presentation points

Financial statements should be transparent so that nothing consequential is hidden or obscured, but as uncomplicated as possible so that they may be easily understood.

- **Avoid too much detail**
  Detailed analyses of all the individual accounts, even in the smallest parishes, can be confusing. Only make reference to what is material and round all figures to the nearest pound.

- **Summarise where possible**
  Summarising different funds in columnar format gives the reader a better overall picture. It also allows a reduction in the number of comparative figures.

- **If preparing summarised financial statements**
  A non-statutory summary, derived from the full financial statements, may be produced to help parishioners understand the finances. There are no longer any rules about the preparation and publication of such summaries in the Charities SORP 2015, but as best practice this guide recommends that information about both the SOFA and the balance sheet should be included. However, the full Annual Report and financial statements should always be available.

- **Put any necessary detail in the notes wherever possible**
  The reader is less likely to be confused by the details when looking at the overall picture.

1.16 What are trust funds and why are they important?

The parish must track all of the money it is given to show that the donor's wishes have been met. As that money comes into the parish for so many different things and in so many different ways, how can it be tracked? The answer is by using 'funds'; accounting records that record money according to the specific purposes for which it was given.

This way of looking at money is well known to many householders who, for example, receive a weekly wage and in order to 'make ends meet' then allocate it to various needs or 'funds':

- giving to 'good causes'

- food shopping

- mortgage or rent

- utility bills

- clothes

- holidays

- and the little bit left over!

The weekly wage has come into one household but it has been allocated for various purposes.

Now let's look at how 'funds' work in a parish where the 'wages' are the money **given** to us by people who choose to say what the money they have given is to be spent on. For example, in one week:

The normal Sunday collection is received (£450) to keep the parish running, as part of its mission and ministry. It is **unrestricted money for the PCC's general purposes**, to be used in whatever way the PCC decides. As in a household, most of the money given to a parish is unrestricted.

The same week a special collection is also taken for youth work (£250). This time it is clear that the people who donated it expect their money to be used for youth work. It is **restricted money** (under trust law). Not even the PCC or the vicar can give permission for it to be used on anything else.

The parish is grateful to receive a legacy of £50,000 for youth work. The will states that this money must be invested, and only the income (interest or dividends) can be spent. This is **endowed money** and it has been restricted to the youth work, so it can't be used for anything else.

On Monday morning all of the money, a total of £50,700, goes into the bank, and the parish accounts show:

Bank current account receives: £50,700 from giving, and out of this:

- £450 is allocated to the general fund (unrestricted money for spending)

- £250 is allocated to the youth fund (restricted money for spending)

- £50,000 is allocated to the youth endowment fund (restricted money for investing).

All the money your parish receives can be put in one bank account so long as you have recorded to which fund the money belongs. As you spend money you also need to show which fund has been used. for example: whenever money is used for youth work it should normally come out of the youth fund. When the parish electricity bill needs paying it comes out of the general fund.

Finally, if the PCC decides, for example, to spend more on youth work, it can move money from the general fund into a designated fund, in this case the 'youth designated fund'. That money is still unrestricted, so if the roof blows off, the PCC can undesignate the money, and move it back to the general fund to use for repairing the roof!

For more information on types of trust fund, see Chapter 2.

chapter 2

Principles of Trust Funds: Accounting and Reporting

2.1 Responsibility

It is clear that the PCC should account in full for its incoming resources and for the way those resources are expended, but in many parishes it is not easy to identify just what the PCC is legally responsible for.

One of the principles of the charity accounting regime is that the charity trustees (here, the PCC members) should identify and include in their annual financial statements any resources that form part of their charity under ecclesiastical or trust law or that it controls and can benefit from.

The following are examples of situations that might arise. What are being described are organisations that may be connected with the church and whose funds may be under the control of the PCC to its own benefit in some way:

- The PCC may have parochial organisations (such as a men's group, a mother and toddlers group, or a church hall management committee) that operate as a part of the local church and are not controlled by another body (such as the Mothers' Union or the Girl Guides). The members may pay contributions that are used to cover the cost of meetings, refreshments, duplicating and speakers' expenses. The organisation may make a contribution to the PCC for the use of a meeting room or for the cost of heating and lighting.

- The PCC may also have funds belonging to it that are administered by members of the congregation, such as a flower fund to cover the cost of flowers in church or a choir fund with some of the money received for weddings.

- There may also be a 'friends' organisation or a parochial trust to which parishioners are invited to contribute.

- There may also be various other trusts, perhaps with the vicar and churchwardens as trustees, and with the passage of time the control of the funds may have appeared to move to the PCC or the purpose of the funds may have become uncertain (these may commonly be called 'vicar and wardens' trusts). The financial statements should include all the money and other assets entrusted to the PCC for whatever purpose, and show how they have been expended during the year and how the unexpended balance of each fund was held at the year end.

  In all of these cases it is necessary to determine whether the income and costs belong to the PCC or to a separate charity or to a separate non-accountable body (e.g. a club or perhaps a 'corporation sole').

2.2 Is the PCC responsible? Questions to ask

Question 1

- Is this group so constituted that it is in law a 'special trust' of the PCC? (A special trust in section 287 of the Charities Act 2011 is defined as 'assets which are held and administered by or on behalf of a charity for any special purposes of the charity, and is so held and administered on separate trusts relating only to that property'.)

- If not, go to the next question.

Question 2

Does the PCC control the group? Related questions that may help to tease out the relationship concern whether the group has a separate constitution; whether it recognises the authority of the PCC; whether the group is a separate charitable institution. Using the church's name and registration with HMRC for reclaiming tax brings it under the PCC's control but just using the church's name in the group's title does not.

Question 3

Is the group under the control of some of the members of the PCC and are they acting as a sub-committee of the PCC in their control? If the PCC members outnumber the others in the control of the group, then the group is under the control of the PCC. The incumbent acting as a member of the PCC under its delegation may fulfil this function. For example, if the incumbent can restructure the control of the group, it is then appropriate to ask whether the incumbent is acting (i) in his/her own right or (ii) on behalf of the PCC. (It should be noted that the incumbent may be three bodies in one, with different capacities: acting in his/her own right as a person; acting alone as a 'corporation sole'; acting in a representative capacity as chair of the PCC.)

If i), then it has been established that the group is not under the control of the full PCC.

- If other PCC members are involved in controlling the group, the same question should be asked: i.e. are they acting (i) in their own right or (ii) on behalf of the PCC as a delegated committee?

- If (i), then it has been established that the group is not under the control of the full PCC.

  If other PCC members are involved in controlling the group, the same question should be asked: i.e. are they acting (i) in their own right or (ii) on behalf of the PCC as a delegated committee?

- If (ii), then you are back to the answer to Question 2.

- If (i), then the question must be asked whether both sides think it is a connected charity – it is going to be 'connected' only by having parallel, common or related objects *and* being administered either in common with the PCC or by common trustees.

2.3 Applying the tests in practice

The following are examples of conclusions drawn from applying the tests:

- Funds raised using the PCC's charitable status to reclaim tax must be included within the PCC's financial statements. This applies to activities, such as a mission gift day, when the money will eventually be given away outside the parish.

- Monies collected by parochial activities, such as women's or men's groups that are not associated with a parent organisation and are not under the control of the PCC, need not be included. However, each organisation should be encouraged to account for its income to its members.

If the PCC underwrites such activities (i.e. pays the bills if the organisers cannot) then they are within PCC control if the organisers cannot show otherwise – e.g. that the PCC only guarantees their creditworthiness but does not make decisions for them or claim their assets as its own.

- Monies that are collected by parochial organisations that are associated with a third party parent organisation, such as the Mothers' Union, are not included. These sums will be dealt with as a part of the financial statements of that organisation and any contribution made to the PCC for the use of meeting rooms will be received and recorded by the PCC, probably as a donation or as income from the letting of facilities. Those organisations should be disclosed in the Annual Report, explaining their relationship as associated charities working with the PCC in some way.

- Monies, restricted either as to their use or to their purpose, that have historically been collected by and from members of the congregation: usually these resources have been handled totally separately from the PCC accounts and the interest of the PCC treasurer is considered to be an intrusion. However, they are and should be accounted for, as restricted income of the PCC.

- A 'friends' organisation that raises funds for the upkeep of the church buildings: if the organisation is a registered charity, it will normally (especially if the PCC is not registered) account separately and file its own returns to the Charity Commission, but it will need to be mentioned in the PCC's Annual Report as a connected charity. If it is treated as an excepted charity under the umbrella of the PCC, then it is a branch and its accounts should be included with the PCC's financial statements.

A 'friends' or other charitable organisation that is not under the PCC's 'umbrella' might not have its own charity registration number. If it has exclusively charitable purposes and a gross income below the registration threshold (currently £5,000 a year), it is not required to register with the Commission but (if only to prove its charitable status) it should still have a written constitution and, like any other charity, must prepare annual accounts and behave charitably. If its income is above the registration threshold, then those managing it are in breach of charity law and should correct this by either registering as an autonomous charity or coming under the control of the PCC.

The PCC should not include in its own (entity*) financial statements the income or expenditure of a separately accountable, independent registered charity associated with the church (possibly the friends) – but the Charities SORP requires any material transactions between a related party and the PCC or any of its connected charities to be disclosed in the accounts notes. However, if the friends settle any PCC bills directly, that amounts to either 'donated services/facilities' or a grant to the PCC, which if Accruals accounts are prepared will then need to be accounted for as an incoming resource and as an appropriate expenditure. (*This means as distinct from group consolidated accounts, which are mandatory under the Charities Act 2011 only for groups exceeding £1m gross income – see Chapter 10.)

The specific accounting policies for any significant categories of income should be explained on the Accruals basis of accounting.

2.4   What are trusts?

A trust is a device in English common law to enable an appointed person or group of people to manage property (i.e. money and/or other assets) for a purpose specified by the trust's founder. The trust deed sets out how the trustees (of which there must normally be at least two, if individuals) shall manage or dispense the assets of the trust. Not all trusts are charitable. To be charitable the trust must have a purpose that is exclusively charitable in law and is for the public benefit.

There may be a variety of charitable trusts within the parish. In order to account correctly for these it will be necessary to identify and classify them. This may require some work depending on how carefully they have been administered in the past (although it should only need to be done once). However, accounting requirements apart, it is important to ensure that property held on trust is administered by the right trustees and used for the right purpose.

There may be some trusts that are not part of or connected with the PCC an will be subject to the normal registration and accounting regimes as with any other charity. These could include:

- The trust of a church school site and associated endowments held by trustees other than the PCC (e.g. the vicar and churchwardens).

- Other educational trusts not held by the PCC. Some parishes have Sunday school or religious education funds created by orders under section 554 of the Education Act 1996. These 'three-fourteenths' trusts arise from the proceeds of sale of former church school sites. It was traditional for the incumbent to have use of the school for half Saturday and all Sunday – hence three-fourteenths – and the church school used the premises for the rest of the time. When the school is closed, three-fourteenths can remain in the parish, normally under the trusteeship of the vicar and churchwardens (which was the traditional pattern for church school trusteeship). The trust, if it has an income over £5,000, will normally have to be registered in its own right and publicly accounted for by its trustees under the normal charity accounting rules. It is not 'a hidden pot of gold' which can be appropriated for the PCC's general purposes.

- Other vicar and churchwardens' trusts will also be separate charities unless they are special trusts of the PCC (see paragraph 2.5).

Then there will be charitable trusts that are or may be connected with the PCC. They may simply have to be accounted for as one of the three main types of PCC fund, but it may be that they need to be 'tidied up' first to clarify what they are for, or that something can be done to make their administration more straightforward. Trusts in this category may be special trusts or they may be controlled charities of the PCC. The former are trusts of property held and administered by or on behalf of the PCC on separate trusts for any special purposes of the PCC:

- the property must be held on separate trusts (as could arise with a gift or legacy);

- it must be held and administered by or on behalf of the PCC, and so the trustees may not necessarily be the PCC itself;

- it must be held for a special purpose of the PCC and so a mere coincidence of objects is not sufficient – the trust must be for a part of the purpose of the PCC.

Therefore, a trust held by the vicar and churchwardens for general ecclesiastical purposes in the parish would not be a special trust of the PCC even though the PCC could also use its general funds for these purposes, but a trust held by the vicar and churchwardens for the express purpose of assisting the PCC in the maintenance of the churchyard would be a special trust of the PCC.

Sometimes, after carrying out all reasonable investigations, it will prove difficult or impossible to classify a particular trust or fund. If the amount involved is large it may be necessary to involve professional advisers to clarify the terms of the trust. However, if the amount is small so that the cost of unravelling the trust terms would be out of proportion to the value of its assets, parishes may wish to adopt a common sense approach and account for the trust as a special trust of the PCC or a controlled 'charity branch', so that at least it is accounted for somewhere.

2.5 Special Trusts

A special trust in section 287 of the Charities Act 2011 is defined as 'assets which are held and administered by or on behalf of a charity for any special purposes of the charity, and is so held and administered on separate trusts relating only to that property'.

2.6 Vicar and churchwardens' trusts

Trusts where the vicar and churchwardens are trustees generally fall into three categories:

Trusts for ecclesiastical purposes

E.g. maintenance of the church and churchyard: these are already required to be vested in the Diocesan Board of Finance (DBF) as custodian trustee. They will have similar objects to those of the PCC and will be included in the PCC's accounts.

Trusts for educational purposes

E.g. Sunday school funds arising from the sale of a church school: these are registered with the Department for Education. They are entirely separate from the PCC's financial statements; however, there may be cases where as 'connected charities' the existence of such charities is disclosable in the PCC's Annual Report, describing the relationship (e.g. the vicar is on both boards etc.) for the information of parishioners.

Trusts for the relief of poverty

E.g. to provide food or clothing for poor people in the parish: unless they are very small these should already be registered with the Charity Commission. Again, they are entirely separate from the PCC's financial statements; however, there may be cases where as 'connected charities' the existence of such charities is disclosable in the PCC's Annual Report, describing the relationship (e.g. the vicar is on both boards etc.) for the information of parishioners.

These trusts will normally need to be shown as a part of the PCC's financial statements. In exceptional circumstances they will need to be disclosed as 'connected charities' in the PCC's Annual Report and the relationship explained – in terms of any trustees and purposes in common and how the trust's activities dovetail with those of the PCC.

It should be noted that where incumbents and churchwardens, as the charity trustees of these trusts, have a legal responsibility to account publicly for them, any member of the public can ask for a copy of the statutory financial statements of such trusts.

2.7 What are funds and fund types?

Funds are the way in which Charity law requires you to track money given by your donors or received from other sources. Why is the government interested in this? They want people to be confident that the money they give for good causes is not misused or wasted but properly used. And, it is hoped, people will then continue to give!

People give to the church for all sorts of reasons. To help track the proper use of restricted money it is allocated to a fund of that type.

Most of the money a PCC receives will be for spending on the PCC's normal activities. This money is 'unrestricted income'. Sometimes the giver will specify particular activities that they wish the money to be used for. This money is 'restricted income'. Occasionally money may be given for the PCC to retain rather than spend on activities. This money is 'endowment capital'.

If you have unrestricted funds that the PCC want to use for a particular purpose, the chosen amount can be earmarked as an unrestricted 'designated fund' for that particular purpose. Each time you receive or spend money you need to say which fund it is for.

The following are examples of the names of some of these funds:

General fund	Bell fund
Church restoration fund	Choir and organ fund
Church hall fund	Legacies fund
General bequest fund	Sunday school fund
Building fund	Mission and charities fund
Fabric fund	Churchyard fund
Flower fund	Maintenance reserve fund

In addition, there may be funds in the name of the person who gave or left the money, possibly for a particular purpose.

Each of these funds is associated with a particular purpose or, in the case of some legacies, with the source of the funds. But the fund names do not immediately tell the reader of the financial statements whether they are held by the PCC on trust for a restricted purpose.

The word 'fund' has an additional use in charity accounting. As well as referring to money allocated by the PCC itself out of its general-purpose funds to be set aside for a particular use (e.g. fixed assets needed for the PCC to function) or project (e.g. to fund the provision of childcare or visits to special-needs parishioners), it is also used where the money is restricted in some way by the donor or by the terms of an appeal. With this latter meaning, each such fund is restricted by trust law, being either income that must be spent only on a specified purpose or else being capital (endowment) in nature that must be retained for the PCC's own use or for investment. In the latter case the investment income may or may not be restricted to spending on a specified purpose. It is important to know the difference between these types of fund as PCCs have to observe clear distinctions between them.

As stated above, many PCCs will already distinguish between all their funds by reference to the purpose to which they have been earmarked (such as those in the list above) or are restricted by law. For some, a clarification will be needed to record properly whether the fund is restricted (and if so, whether it is endowed) and for what purpose, or else unrestricted (and, if so, to confirm its status if designated for a particular purpose) in order to be able to demonstrate that the PCC has properly exercised the trust placed in it.

The charity accounting framework requires fund-based financial statements that in any case enable the reader to see that the PCC is spending its funds on the purposes for which they have been given. It may be helpful for smaller PCCs to give the project-based information, which is not required by law below the statutory audit threshold, as well as the funding aspect – i.e. surplus or deficit, either in a note to the financial statements or in the Annual Report (e.g. 'sales of the parish magazine exceeded printing costs by £140'). Even if not given in the financial statements, such information is likely to be important for the PCC in carrying out its responsibilities, and thus it may be appropriate to report such information in the 'Performance and Achievements' section of the Annual Report.

The following table shows what each type of fund is and how it can be used:

The fund type	Where the money comes from	How it can be used	Where it can be banked	Who decides how the money is used
Unrestricted income: The general fund	Normal Sunday or other collections with no special purpose Gifts for the Parish Gift days for the general work of the parish Grants for the general work of the parish Money given for use at the vicar or PCC's discretion	For the upkeep of the parish For purposes agreed by the PCC For the parish share For giving to other appeals or charities	In any bank or deposit account so long as it has been recorded as allocated to the general fund	The PCC

Unrestricted designated funds It remains unrestricted money but is allocated for a particular purpose	It is money given to the general fund that the PCC has allocated for a particular purpose	Only for the purpose decided by the PCC	In any bank or deposit account so long as it has been recorded as allocated to a designated fund	The PCC
Restricted income: Funds given to the PCC to be spent for a specific purpose	Special collections, gifts and donations, appeals, gift days or legacies where the PCC or the donor has indicated that the money will be used for a specific purpose (even if only in response to a PCC appeal for that purpose)	Only for the purpose for which it was given	In any bank or deposit account so long as it has been recorded as allocated to the correct restricted fund	The donor (at the time of gift) or the terms of the appeal (or in certain situations the Charity Commission), or the PCC with Charity Commission consent
Endowment capital: Funds given to the PCC for longer-term retention rather than immediate spending The capital may be permanent or expendable and its use can be unrestricted or purposes restricted by the donor	Legacies, capital gifts or grants, capital appeals – whether of money for investment, or of investment assets or non-investment assets for the PCC's own use	Only for the benefit of the PCC, and restricted to any special purpose for which it was given	In any deposit or investment account so long as it has been recorded as allocated to the general or specific endowment fund as appropriate	The donor (at the time of gift) or the terms of the appeal (if the donor has not indicated that they can only be used for something specific, then the PCC decides)

Hints and tips

Where possible use restricted money first. For example, if you have a youth restricted fund and the bill you are paying is for a youth event, it is likely that you can use this fund.

Why is this important? Restricted money can only be used for the purpose for which it was first given. Using restricted money when you can will leave more money in your general fund. This will give you the greatest flexibility to meet whatever happens later in the year!

When having a gift day or appeal, if possible make it for the general work of the church – this will give you the most flexibility when using the money.

If you have a specific appeal or gift day, make it clear that any extra money will be put into the general fund. For example, if you have an appeal for the roof which is so successful that the roof is repaired with £500 left over unless you have told people that any extra money will go to the general fund, this £500 must remain in the roof restricted fund.

Telling people what you will do if you get too much money (or if so little money that the project has to be aborted) means that they are fully aware of how their money will be used and so have the choice. It will also avoid having restricted money, that you cannot use.

When you claim Gift Aid on donations it must go to the fund to which the original money was given. This means that if a person gives you money for the youth work in the church it is restricted to youth work, and so is any Gift Aid you claim on that money.

2.8 Unrestricted funds

All PCCs have a general-purpose income fund, normally called a general fund, which they use to pay all the everyday expenses. This fund is 'unrestricted' because the money has been given to the church on the general understanding that it will be used at the discretion of the PCC for furthering the mission and ministry of the church. Unless specified otherwise, all the money received by the church is put into the general fund. Income generated from assets held in an unrestricted fund will be unrestricted income.

The PCC may decide to put some of the unrestricted fund money aside in other funds for use in the future (for example, for future building repairs). This money is 'designated' for these particular projects for administration purposes only. Designated funds are still unrestricted and can be moved to other general funds (redesignated or undesignated) if the PCC so decides. It is also important to bear in mind that these designated funds cannot at any time exceed the total amount of the general fund – i.e. you cannot earmark money for future spending before you get it, so they cannot leave you with a negative figure for the general fund's 'free reserves' (i.e. undesignated monies) but must be capped if necessary to avoid that. This is important because of the requirement to disclose in the Annual Report the trustees' policy on reserves, the actual reserves level at the year end and what is being done to bridge any gap between the aimed-for and actual levels of free reserves.

2.9 Restricted funds

PCCs also receive money that has been given for a particular purpose, for example:

● a collection in church may be announced as being for a particular purpose (such as the purchase of new hymn books or the repair of the tower);

● a fundraising event (such as a rummage sale or a coffee morning) may be held for a particular purpose;

● a donation may have been made or a legacy may have been left to the church for a particular purpose (such as the upkeep of the churchyard or the repair of the fabric).

All these sums have been restricted by the donor for a particular purpose and unless the donor has specifically reserved a right of consent to variation of purpose they cannot, and must not, be used by the PCC for any other purpose unless determined by the courts or the Charity Commission or else, for small trusts, the purpose is varied under the statutory powers given to trustees in the 2011 Act. Income generated from assets held in a restricted fund will generally be subject to the same restrictions as the fund the asset belongs to (unless the donor has specified otherwise).

An oral or written appeal or a collection for a special purpose, such as the fabric fund, will restrict the income to that purpose. There may be times when more money is raised than is needed for the particular purpose of the appeal. This excess money is restricted to the purpose and should be retained for use for the same purpose, or returned to the donors (except under the Gift Aid Scheme, which prohibits refunds).

This situation can be eased if the PCC acquires the power beforehand to use any surpluses for other purposes. The easiest way to avoid any problem is by announcing at the time of the appeal that any unused balance will be put to the general purposes of the PCC unless a donor explicitly forbids this (which would be a rarity). The restriction then applies until the purpose of the appeal has been satisfied. (A general notice to this effect can be placed prominently in the church to catch all occasions.) If someone wants to make a significant donation for a particular purpose, the donor could be invited to specify that they give the PCC permission to use it or a surplus for general or alternative specific purposes under certain conditions.

There could also be a potential problem if insufficient funds are raised for a particular purpose and the shortfall cannot be made good out of general funds. The PCC should always make clear in appeals what it would do if this situation were to lead to the project being abandoned – for example, to return all the donations (except where this is prohibited under the Gift Aid rules) or to use them for another related purpose.

When special collections (including any Gift Aid) are made to send straight off to other charities (e.g. Christian Aid, missionary societies) and the nature of the appeal is that there is no discretion for the PCC to do anything other than send the money directly to the charity, these are not funds of the PCC, as it is acting only as a collecting agent, and so the appeal should not be included in the PCC's gross income or total expenditure. It is good practice to include a list of these collections in the PCC's Annual Report, if only to confirm to the congregation that all appeals money collected has been duly passed on to the intended charity.

2.10 Endowment funds

Another form of restricted fund is known as an endowment. This is either capital money given to the church as permanent or (alternatively) expendable* capital with the specific instruction that only the income gained from investing the money can be spent, or it is a capital asset (such as a house) donated to be retained for continuing use by the church. (*If the donor has in any way authorised the spending of capital, it will be an 'expendable' endowment to the extent of the trustees' discretionary power to spend it.) The original money or assets (the 'capital') cannot be spent as income unless so authorised and must remain in the form of equivalent fixed assets (such as a house) or investments, but not necessarily the same asset that was given. It may be in a fund that is named after the donor.

There are thus two types of endowment capital, which must be distinguished in accruals accounts by note:

2.10.1 permanent:

a particular type of restricted fund where the capital, in accordance with the explicit requirements of the founding donor, must be held permanently. Any income return generated by the invested endowment (e.g. dividends) must be spent as originally determined by the donor, whereas any investment holding or disposal gain (less losses) belongs to capital on the same terms as the original gift.

2.10.2 expendable:

an endowment fund where the capital may, in certain circumstances, be spent. The PCC have this power, if given or implied by the donor. This fund is not income when it is first received, because there is no intermediate duty on the part of the PCC to spend it for its intended purposes. The PCC has the legal right (and even the duty) to retain the capital as capital and a further legal right to convert capital into income in accordance with the express or implied terms of trust imposed by the donor. However, if the power to convert is used, then at that time the amount converted becomes income. Any income return generated by the invested endowment will be required by law to be spent as determined by the donor without unreasonable delay and so cannot just be added to the retained capital unless a specific legal power to 'accumulate' income as capital allows this. Any investment holding or disposal gains (less losses) belong to capital on the same terms as the original gift.

Any expenses incurred in the administration of the capital fund (such as the fees of the person who manages the investments) should be charged against the capital of the fund unless the founding donor clearly intended otherwise. However, if the trust establishing a fund provides for it or if the capital fund has insufficient liquid assets to meet such costs (e.g. they cannot be used, as they consist only of land or buildings needed for the PCC's own use), the expenses can be charged to income (normally to the general fund).

2.11 Accounting for different types of fund

Where a PCC holds trust funds other than unrestricted funds, its accounting records must be adequate to allow separate accounts to be produced for each distinct trust fund. Restricted income funds and endowment capital funds must be shown separately in the annual financial statements. PCCs should also show in the accounts notes (if not in the balance sheet) how any designated funds have moved between year ends.

In the accounting records this administrative separation to comply with trust law can be done either by using separate columns in the cash book for the different types of trust fund or by clearly labelling each entry to distinguish those that are unrestricted and those that are restricted as to capital or as to income or merely designated.

In the annual financial statements unrestricted, restricted and endowment funds must be reported separately. As a minimum all funds of one type should be reported together, either as three separate columns (i.e. Receipts and Payments Accounts example) or, in the case of accounts on the Receipts and Payments basis, alternatively as separate statements of account. It is important that the reader can tell that the funds are not all held on the same legal basis and it is important that the PCC members know that certain funds have restrictions on the way the money can be used. The PCC must also be able to demonstrate that it still holds assets belonging to restricted and endowment funds and has not used these for unauthorised spending, nor for unauthorised purposes. It is a breach of trust to spend restricted income funds for purposes other than those for which they were given without the prior consent of the Charity Commission, or to spend trust capital without proper authority.

The PCC's unused monies, unless held for immediate spending, may need to be invested and investment returns generated. Any holding gains/losses and income earned belong to the fund whose assets were invested and so the income is subject to the same restrictions of purpose as apply to that fund. Therefore, the investment returns must be identified for each different fund, and in the case of investment pooling* this must be based on the amounts invested by each fund and the time for which they were invested, and then accounted for as part of the fund to which have belonged from the outset. (*Statutory authority for this is provided by the Trustee Act 2000.)

The only exceptions to this are:

- where the donor has expressly provided for some other use for the investment income;

- where the asset is part of a permanent endowment held for general purposes. In this case the capital is restricted in an endowment fund (because it cannot be spent) but the income is unrestricted since it can (and normally must) be spent for the PCC's general purposes or for any designated purpose.

If an endowment fund has assets (e.g. a house or investments) and any are sold, the proceeds of sale must be held within the same endowment fund. The same applies to the sale of investment securities belonging to a restricted income fund.

The SORP makes it clear that funds may be grouped and sub-analysed by major fund in the notes to the financial statements, and so all endowments may be reported on as one group, all other restricted funds as another group and all funds with no such restriction as a third group. It also requires the SOFA, balance sheet and any cash flow statement to show comparative figures for every item shown therein. PCCs have the option either to show the fund-accounting comparatives for all figures shown in the SOFA (using extra columns to do so) or else to show them in a 'prominent' accounts note.

In some cases other bodies of trustees may hold funds from which the PCC is legally entitled to benefit. If such trustees are only the custodians (i.e. they have no discretion over the use of the fund) then that money is a fund (in most cases an endowment fund) of the PCC. If the PCC does not have enough discretion over the use of funds held in its name to make it the 'charity trustee' of those funds, then they should not be accounted for in the PCC's financial statements. Instead, the fact of the fund's existence, its purpose and a description of the assets belonging to it should be disclosed in the PCC's Annual Report as custodian trusteeship holding, together with how the connected charity's activity relates to that of the PCC and how the necessary segregation of assets is maintained.

With parishes bearing an increasingly larger part of the costs of maintaining the Church of England it may seem odd to think that there may be parishes who have received income that they may find difficult to spend. Usually these will relate to restricted funds. Some examples might include the following:

- The PCC has investments in a restricted fund that are the proceeds of a house used for curates and parish staff in the past. This may be from a period in between employment of one staff member and another when a house has been bought in which it is possible that the parish is subsequently not required to house a worker; the PCC will then have to consider what to do with the fund.

- A building appeal fund has been set up but the proper permissions have not yet been granted and there is some doubt whether the project will go ahead.

- Money has been specifically raised to send an individual to undertake a specific project in a third-world country but because of a recent civil war that person cannot go or that project is stalled.

The status of such funds should be explained in the notes to the financial statements and any proposed action to dispose of the unexpended balances should be disclosed. This may include returning funds to the donors (subject to Gift Aid scheme rules) or obtaining permission (either from the donors (if, unusually, they had reserved to themselves a power of variation of the terms of trust) or by order of the Charity Commission) for the funds to be spent on other purposes.

Tips for handling different funds

- Clear records of restricted money should be kept so that it can readily be identified. Poor records can lead to confused administration and then it is possible that the rules will be ignored and restricted and unrestricted funds will be unlawfully merged with one another.

- Expenditure of restricted funds may anticipate promised funding at the time the expenditure is incurred. It is acceptable practice in such cases to show a deficit on the project and then wait for the promised funding before deciding what balance must be met from the general fund. However, any insufficiency of the general fund for this purpose cannot be made good out of other restricted funds. Where material, deficit balances on restricted funds should be shown separately on the face of the balance sheet, and not netted off against other restricted fund balances. Details of how the deficit is to be eliminated will also need to be given in the Annual Report (see Chapter 3).

- Collections at some funerals are taken in a bowl by the church door and are taken by the undertaker for a specific purpose at the wish of the bereaved family. These collections should only be recorded and accounted for by the PCC if the money is given directly to the church or the PCC makes the decision as to the use to which it should be put.

- Fees collected by the PCC (in the 'agency' capacity) for the services of bell ringers, organists, vergers or choir at weddings and similarly for organists, vergers and gravediggers at funerals (as with the collection of and fees belonging to the diocesan board of finance), should not be included in the financial statements if the money is paid over in full directly to those involved. In this case the PCC is acting as an intermediary and these fees do not count towards PCC income. PCCs will from time to time collect money on behalf of other charities in a public place or in church services. Examples of this include Christmas carolling and Christian Aid door-to-door collections. In these instances these receipts are not to be included in the PCC's income as the PCC is acting as an agent for the other charity. This is the case whether the money collected is sent off to the charity or if the money is counted and the PCC treasurer writes out a cheque for money paid into its bank account.

- PCCs should remember that they do not have to accept a gift if they are uncertain of its source or if they are not happy at abiding by the donor's conditions. All gifts for which the PCC reclaims tax under the Gift Aid scheme must be shown in the financial statements and its use agreed by the PCC. This would include the situation where tax is reclaimed on a donation paid under Gift Aid to be used for the PCC's charitable purposes at the minister's discretion.

- Legacies given for the general purposes of the PCC should immediately be credited to the general fund. Unless the donor has restricted the use of the legacy in the will, it remains unrestricted and may not be restricted by the PCC. All or a part of the legacy may then be designated for a particular purpose but it should not be designated to a 'legacy fund' with no intention as to its use.

- The separate administration of differently restricted funds does not require them necessarily to be kept in separate bank accounts, but this may be a useful practice in some circumstances as it does guarantee that they can always be identified as such.

- In the past, many parishes have operated with a large number of funds for different aspects of the church's life. Such a large number involves administrative complexity in the accounting system and the published financial statements. PCCs are recommended to keep under review the number of funds while taking care not to conflict with the strict rules on restricted and endowment funds.

- PCCs are advised to ensure that they have proper systems in place for the signing of cheques, the counting of collections (including the opening of planned giving envelopes) and their prompt payment into the bank.

2.12 Tips for handling other church funds

- The treasurer (on behalf of the PCC) should ensure that proper accounting records are kept by PCC 'branches' (organisations and those who hold the purses for small extra funds for which the PCC is accountable in law). Each year the treasurer will need to obtain an accurate return from each 'branch', which can be quite simple, consisting of a summary of Receipts and Payments for the year, and a list of any assets and liabilities at the year end. The figures from these organisations or funds should be added to the PCC's financial statements if they are material.

- Unless these 'branches' are a separately accountable legal entity, all the funds that they hold are the legal property of the PCC, whether or not they have a separate bank account.

- Friends' organisations not under the control of the PCC should be advised to have themselves properly constituted.

- Under the Ecclesiastical Fees (Amendment) Measure 2011, a portion of the parochial fees received is the legal property of the Diocesan Board of Finance with the remaining portion belonging to the PCC. These are separate fees: one forms part of the PCC's income while the other is the DBF's income (unless the fees are not assigned, when they will continue to be declared by the freehold incumbent whose stipend is reduced accordingly). It is therefore important that, when one cheque is received for both types of fee, the treasurer ensures that the relevant portion is paid to the DBF. Guidance to the Measure strongly suggests that in all cases (other than for non-assigned freeholders) incumbents should not handle fees, but that the PCC should be the local agent. The treasurer should not include the DBF's fee as part of PCC income in any way because they are only acting as an agent for the DBF when they collect fees on the DBF's behalf.

2.13 Categories of income and expenditure

Income and endowments

Account description	Receipts & payments category	Account heading	SOFA category	Account heading	RPF note (2016 only)
Gift Aid – bank	Voluntary receipts	Planned giving	Voluntary income	Planned giving	01
Gift Aid – envelopes					01
Other planned giving					02
Loose plate collections		Collections at services		Collections at services	03
Special collections					03
Gift days		All other giving/ voluntary receipts		All other giving/ voluntary income	04
Giving through church boxes					04
Donations appeals etc.					04
Gifts of freehold or leasehold land or of quoted shares/securities at market value	N/A	N/A			04
Legacies					07
Recurring grants					08
Non-recurring one-off grants					08
Donated services and facilities: The quantified 'value to the charity' of donated assistance that the PCC would otherwise have had to purchase to meet its actual needs. Include in the most appropriate category	N/A	N/A			Include in the most appropriate category
Gift Aid recovered This must be shown separately and, if no tax recovery claim has been made, an explanation should be given in a note to the financial statements		Gift Aid recovered		Gift Aid recovered	06
Church fetes, rummage sales, bazaars, etc.	Activities for generating funds	Fund Raising	Activities for generating funds	Fund Raising	09
Bookstall – non-church purposes					12
Church hall lettings – non objects related					12
Parish magazine – advertising					12
Dividends	Investment income	Income from investments	Investment income	Income from investments	10
Bank and building society interest					10
Rent from lands or buildings owned by the PCC					10

Account description	Receipts & payments category	Account heading	SOFA category	Account heading	RPF note (2016 only)
Fees for weddings and funerals	Church Activities	Receipts from church activities	Church activities	Income from church activities	11
Fees for courses, groups and events					11
Bookstall and magazine sales – objects related					12
Church hall lettings – objects related					12
Insurance claims – where the insurer pays a supplier's bill direct that amount might or might not count as income. This depends on the nature of the insurance policy.	Other receipts	Other receipts	Other incoming resources	Other incoming resources	13
Gain on sales of fixed assets held for the PCC's own use – sale proceeds less net book value	N/A	N/A			13
Other incoming resources not covered elsewhere					13

Expenditure

Account description	Receipts & payments category	Account heading	SOFA category	Account heading	RPF note (2016 only)
Parish share/Quota /Family purse	Church activities	Parish share/ Quota/Family purse	Church activities	Parish share/ Quota/Family purse	19
Salaries and wages of parish staff		Clergy and staffing		Clergy and staffing	20
National Insurance of parish staff					20
Pension contributions of parish staff					20
Working expenses of clergy					21
Council tax					21
Parsonage house expenses					21
Water rates – vicarage					21
Clergy telephone					21
Visiting speakers/locums					21
Education		Church running expenses		Church running expenses	22
Parish training and mission					22
Church running – insurance					23
Church office – telephone					23
Organ/piano tuning					23
Church maintenance					23

Account description	Receipts & payments category	Account heading	SOFA category	Account heading	RPF note (2016 only)
Cleaning					23
Upkeep of services					23
Upkeep of churchyard					23
Printing, postage & stationery	Church Activities		Church Activities		23
Church running – depreciation	N/A	N/A			23
Church running – electric, oil & gas					24
Church running – water					24
Magazine & books expenses – PCC objects related					25
Other Church Running Expenses					23
Hall running – oil		Hall Running Costs		Hall Running Costs (& other PCC functional properties)	25
Hall running – electricity					25
Hall running – gas					25
Hall running – insurance					25
Hall running – maintenance					25
Hall running – telephone					25
Hall running – water					25
Hall running – depreciation	N/A	N/A			25
Church major repairs – structure		Church Repairs & Maintenance		Church Repairs & Maintenance	27
Church major repairs – installation					27
Church interior and exterior decorating					27
Hall + major repairs – structure		Hall Repairs & Maintenance		Hall (& other PCC properties) Repairs & Maintenance	28
Hall + major repairs – installation					28
Hall + interior and exterior decorating					28
Other PCC property upkeep					28
Giving to missionary societies		Mission Giving and Donations		Mission Giving and Donations	18
Giving – relief and development agencies					18
Other donations to support wider mission work outside the Parish					18

Account Description	Receipts & payments category	Account heading	SOFA category	Account heading	RPF note (2016 only)
Fees paid to professional fund-raisers	Cost of generating funds	Fundraising activities	Cost of generating funds	Costs of generating voluntary income	17
Costs of applying for grants					17
Costs of stewardship campaign					17
Costs of fetes and other events		Fundraising trading: cost of goods sold and other costs		Fundraising trading: cost of goods sold and other costs	
Bookstall cost of goods for fund-raising purposes and associated running costs					25
Investment management costs		Investment management costs		Investment management costs	
Independent examination (or audit costs)	Governance costs	Independent examination costs	Apportioned, and a note to the accounts (see Chapter 6)		26
Costs of trustee training/PCC meetings		Trustee training			26
Any resources expended that the PCC has not been able to analyse within the other resources expended categories. (Losses on fixed assets should be treated as additional depreciation under the appropriate heading – **only applies to accruals accounting.**)					
The following is a table of additional entries, and their relevant notes, for the Return of Parish Finance					
Purchase of investments					99
Purchase of fixed assets for church purposes					99
Loan repayments					99
Transfers to term deposits					99
Purchase of new staff housing					29
New building work on church					29
New building work on church hall					29
Bank current account					31
CCLA deposit account					31
Cash in hand					31

chapter 3

The Annual Report

Introduction

The preparation of a written Annual Report, like the preparation of the financial statements, is the joint responsibility of the whole PCC. It puts all the PCC's financial statements into perspective and relates them to the wider life of the church. It will review the past year and link financial plans to the vision for the future. For this reason, while it is legally a separate document from the financial statements, the Annual Report and accounts (including the independent examiner/audit report) should always be presented together in the same publication.

The Church Representation Rules (Rule 9(1) (b)) require 'an annual report on the proceedings of the parochial church council and the activities of the parish generally' to be received by the Annual Parochial Church Meeting (APCM). The meeting is then free to discuss it.

The report is quite separate from the statement or address that the incumbent may wish to make to the APCM.

The Church Accounting Regulations 2006 no longer contain specific requirements as to the information to be included in the Annual Report, but simply refer to the need to comply with the Charities Act, any regulations made there under and the current charities SORP. The detailed requirements are in paragraphs 3.1 to 3.10 below.

The report will usually be drafted by the secretary and the treasurer of the PCC, but some PCCs may wish to involve others in the drafting. It is a significant document in the life of the church and should be prepared in that light rather than as a chore to be completed.

The PCC must adopt the report before it is presented to the APCM and it must be dated and signed by the chairman of the PCC meeting at which it was adopted. Ideally an early draft should be shown to the PCC, but beware attempting to draft by committee.

The independent examiner or the auditor will need to see the report as a part of their scrutiny of the financial statements.

Because the report must be written for the general public as well as for church members, it has to include information that church members might take for granted, such as identification of the parish church, how the PCC operates and the names of its members.

The whole report should deal with the main activities of the church and new developments planned. It will give a flavour of the church at worship, 'being' as well as 'doing', through its pastoral ministry and mission outreach, showing how it relates to those outside and on the fringes as well as in the congregation.

It is in no one's interest to make the report long and complicated. It is much more likely to be read if it is succinct and to the point. PCCs that have access to computers and desktop publishing facilities will want to make the layout attractive and may wish to include graphs, graphics and photographs.

The report should explain the governance and management structure and enable the reader to understand how the numerical part of the financial statements relates to the organisational structure and activities of the PCC. (See example included in Chapter 8.)

The full content of the report is recommended as best practice for all PCCs, but for all those PCCs that are below the audit threshold there are significant reductions in the disclosures.

The following sections outline the requirements that all PCCs must report. There are, however, specific mandatory requirements for larger PCCs. These additional reporting requirements (which may still be included by smaller PCCs) are shown in italics at the end of each section.

3.1   Aim and purposes

This section establishes the framework under which the PCC has operated in the year and its intentions. It should provide a statement of the aims and objects of the PCC. The primary object of all PCCs will be the promotion of the gospel of our Lord Jesus Christ according to the doctrines and practices of the Church of England. The PCC (Powers) Measure 1956 states that the PCC 'is to co-operate with the minister in promoting in the parish the whole mission of the Church, pastoral, evangelistic, social and ecumenical'. Some parishes may have 'mission' or 'vision' statements they wish to include.

Although all charities have always had to meet the public benefit requirement, the Charities Act highlights it by requiring all charities to demonstrate, explicitly, that their aims are for the public benefit, including charities advancing education or religion or relieving poverty, which were previously presumed to be for the public benefit.

Public benefit is assessed by two key principles:

1)   There must be an identifiable benefit or benefits.

2)   The benefit must be to the public, or section of the public.

The level of detail the PCC must provide will depend on whether it is a larger or smaller PCC (£500k gross income threshold).

For those below the threshold, the PCC must include a brief summary in its Annual Report of the main activities undertaken, explaining how these furthered the PCC's aims for the public benefit. The summary should also confirm that the PCC has had regard to the Charity Commission public benefit guidance, where relevant. The PCC can, of course, provide fuller public benefit statements if it wishes.

For those above the threshold, the PCC must provide a fuller explanation in their Annual Report of the significant activities undertaken in order to carry out the PCC's aims and strategies. It is up to the PCC to decide how much detail it wants to provide to clearly illustrate what it's charity has done in the reporting year to meet the requirement. The Charity Commission guidance states that 'a charity that said nothing on public benefit in its Trustees' Annual Report, or produced only the briefest statement with no detail, would be in breach of the public benefit reporting requirement.'

Public benefit should be demonstrated in the 'Objectives and activities' and 'Achievements and performance' sections.

3.2   Objectives and activities

This section establishes how the PCC is trying to fulfil the aims of the church. All PCCs should provide a summary of the main objectives and activities of the church in the year. This should include:

- an explanation of the PCC's main objectives for the year. These may, largely, remain constant from year to year, but may also include a particular focus for a year, which may either have been determined by the PCC (such as particular work on the buildings) or led by the deanery or the diocese, (such as mission and growth initiatives).

- an explanation of the strategies and activities that have been adopted to enable the PCC to achieve its objectives. This could provide details of the programmes the church does, such as: regular worship services; house groups; women's, men's and youth groups; drop-in centres; outreach work etc.

- the costs of programmes and activities can be shown in the accounts and thus provide a direct link to the report;

- the policy for making grants or donations should be given (including how potential recipients are identified). It will be rare for a PCC to have social or programme-related investment activities but where these exist the policies adopted for the selection and management of these activities should be given.

- an explanation of the contribution of volunteers where they play a significant role either in the charitable activities of the PCC or in generating funds. This might include an explanation of the activities undertaken and the contribution in terms of hours or staff equivalents and may also include an indicative value of this contribution. Similarly, where the PCC has received unquantifiable free facilities or services during the year, it should explain briefly the extent to which it relies on these continuing in order to pursue its work.

3.3 Achievements and performance

This section details how the PCC should provide a summary of the main achievements of the church in the year. This could include:

- extracts from returns to the diocese on numbers of different types of services held and the attendance at the regular services, baptisms, confirmations, etc.;

- details of the various special activities that the church ran during the year, e.g. missions, fundraising for overseas mission, pilgrimages, community events etc.;

- a review of the charitable activities undertaken that explains the performance achieved against the objectives set. In some cases it will be possible to explain the outcomes in terms of numbers (such as numbers on the electoral roll and/or attendance figures). Much of the work of the church, however, cannot be reduced to numbers and in order to evaluate its achievements the PCC will need to draw on reports of experiences, which may be oral or written;

- where the objectives set cover a longer term than the financial year, the review will take the form of a progress report;

- where they are material, a review of the performance of fundraising activities against the objectives set for them;

- where material investments are held, details of investment performance against the investment objectives set;

- a commentary on those factors within and outside the PCC's control that are relevant to the achievement of the objectives. These might include relationships with employees, members of the congregation, and the church's position in the wider community. This is intended to give a context to the activities of the year. For example, the departure of the incumbent or a key member of staff may, necessarily, curtail some of the work planned for the year.

3.4 Financial review

The report will paint a picture of the financial position of the PCC that will supplement the financial statements. They will assist the reader in understanding what it is that they are being asked to support financially and how those resources (and others) are being stewarded and used. More specifically, as a new disclosure requirement for all charities says: 'If, at the date of approving the report and accounts, there are uncertainties about the [PCC's] ability to continue as a going concern, the nature of these uncertainties should be explained.' For any fund or subsidiary undertaking that is materially in deficit, the circumstances giving rise to the deficit and the steps being taken to eliminate the deficit must be explained.

It should also review the financial position of any subsidiary undertakings the church may have. This section of the report should also include:

- an explanation of the circumstances that have given rise to any fund that is materially in deficit and details of any steps being taken to eliminate that deficit;

- details of the principal funding sources and how expenditure in the year under review has supported the key objectives of the PCC;

- where material investments are held, the investment policy and objectives, including the extent to which social, environmental or ethical considerations are taken into account.

3.5 Reserves policy

The PCC should formulate and disclose its policy on reserves. The adoption of a policy on reserves will help to identify situations where a PCC may need to consider either reducing or increasing the level of reserves that it holds. For example, the church may be in receipt of income that more than covers all its running costs (including diocesan parish share). Money collected from parishioners is therefore over and above what the parish needs. Alternatively, there may be parishes where the reserves are too low to cope with the requirements of the PCC's cash flow.

In addition to stating the amount of reserves held, the report should explain what the PCC considers to be an appropriate level of free reserves, and what action the PCC proposes to take to reduce or increase its free reserves where necessary. This will show the parish that it is acting responsibly in holding the level of reserves that it holds. The public can then fully understand the availability and planned use of the PCC's funds. Even if the PCC has no free reserves, it should provide an explanation.

Free reserves are defined as that part of the PCC's income funds that is freely available. This definition of reserves therefore normally excludes:

(a) permanent endowment funds;

(b) expendable endowment funds;

(c) restricted income funds;

(d) any part of unrestricted funds that is not currently available for spending (e.g. income funds that can only be realised by disposing of fixed assets held for charity use).

Individual parishes may have more or less reserves than this simple calculation suggests. For example, they may have expendable endowments that can be spent (increasing reserves) or they may have designated some part of general funds for a particular project (reducing reserves). For larger PCCs the reserves-level disclosure is more comprehensive. It should:

- state the amount of the total funds the charity holds at the year end;

- identify the amount of any funds that are restricted and not available for general purposes of the PCC at the year end;

- identify and explain any material amounts that have been designated or otherwise committed as at the year end;

- indicate the likely timing of the expenditure of any material amounts designated or otherwise committed at the year end;

- identify the amount of any fund that can only be realised by disposing of tangible fixed assets or programme-related investments;

- state the amount of reserves the PCC holds at the year end after deducting any restricted or designated funds;

- compare the amount of reserves with the PCC's reserves policy and explain, where relevant, what steps it is taking to bring the amount of reserves it holds into line with the level of reserves identified by the trustees as appropriate given their plans for the future activities of the PCC.

3.6 Funds held as custodian trustees on behalf of others

In some circumstances the PCC may act as a custodian trustee for the assets of another charity. Where this is the case the report should give: a brief description of the assets held; the name and objects of the charity on whose behalf they are held and an explanation of how this fits with the objects of the PCC; details of the arrangements for the safe custody and segregation of such assets from those of the PCC.

3.7 Plans for future periods

The Annual Report should provide the reader with an explanation of the PCC's plans for the future (this will be the current year at the time the report is presented), including the key objectives and activities planned to support them. These will then form the basis of the objectives and activities section of the next report.

3.8 Risk management

Larger PCCs (with a gross income of more than £500,000) are required to make a risk-management statement. However, it is best practice for all PCCs to be aware of their major risks and it is strongly recommended that all PCCs have a risk-management policy.

PCCs must include in their Annual Report 'a description of the principal risks and uncertainties facing the charity and its subsidiary undertakings, as identified by the charity trustees [PCC members], together with a summary of their plans and strategies for managing those risks', as well as 'any factors that are likely to affect the financial performance or position going forward'.

For further details on risk management see the Charity Commission Guidance CC26, which is available on its website.

3.9 Structure, governance and management

This section should make clear to the reader the legal framework within which the PCC operates, and how decisions are made. It should include:

- An explanation of how the PCC is constituted. For most PCCs this will be as shown below. However, a PCC that is a team ministry or part of a united benefice should briefly outline how it is established here.

  'The Parochial Church Council is a corporate body established by the Church of England. The PCC operates under the Parochial Church Council Powers Measure. The PCC is a Registered Charity (or where the PCC has gross income under £100,000 and is not a registered charity – 'The PCC is excepted by order from registering with the Charity Commission').'

- A statement that the appointment of PCC members is governed by and set out in the Church Representation Rules.

- If the PCC has any related trusts or charities, an explanation of the relationship of the PCC to these trusts.

- The policies and procedures adopted for the recruitment, induction and training of PCC members. As the PCC has ultimate responsibility for a wide range of matters affecting the parish, including such matters as compliance with health and safety, disability discrimination legislation and child protection, it is important that the PCC adopts appropriate training procedures. These are likely to include training courses arranged by the diocese or deanery that are attended by a PCC representative who reports back to the PCC as a body, and the dissemination of reading matter.

- A brief description of the way the PCC organises itself in order to carry out its aims and objectives.

- Many PCCs will probably have only a standing committee, but others may well have various committees. The purpose or terms of reference of the committees should be summarised. This should make clear the types of decision that are delegated to committees or to the incumbent or administrator.

- The arrangements for setting the pay and remuneration of the PCC's key management personnel and any benchmarks, parameters or criteria used in setting their pay.

3.10 Administrative information

This information should be given each year, even though much of it may be the same as for the previous year; it may be recorded separately from the main body of the report:

- the full name (town/village and church dedication) of the PCC;

- the location of the church (or address if it has one) and the PCC correspondence address. This could be the church office (if there is one), that of the incumbent or of an officer of the PCC that can be made public;

- the charity registration number (where applicable);

- the names of all the members of the PCC who have served since the commencement of the financial year until the approval of the financial statements. The names of those who have left the PCC and the names of those who have replaced them should be given. This is a list of all those who have been trustees of the charity. Those who have been officers of the PCC should be indicated;

- the names and addresses of bankers, legal and other advisers to the PCC, and of the independent examiner or auditor;

- the name of the person or persons to whom day-to-day management is delegated, e.g. the incumbent, and (for larger PCCs) any other persons designated as 'key management personnel'.

chapter 4

Receipts and Payments Accounting

4.1 What is Receipts and Payments account?

As the name suggests, it is a way of summarising all receipts (the cash coming into the parish, such as Sunday giving, special collections, other gifts of money etc.) and all payments (the cash going out of the parish, such as electricity, parish share, giving to other good causes etc.). To give a full picture, it also needs to list the assets (owned by the PCC) and liabilities (owed by the PCC) at the year end.

All Church of England parishes must have a financial year that is the calendar year: 1 January to 31 December (see the Church Representation Rules).

The annual report and accounts has four components that you need to provide at the end of the year.

1. Trustees' Annual Report

2. A Receipts and Payments account (for each fund)

3. A Statement of Assets and Liabilities

4. Independent examiner's report on the accounts

> To see how these reports work in practice we have provided an example for a fictitious church – St Emillion's.

The Charity Commission sets the ground rules for the design and content of the Trustees' Annual Report and the independent examiner's report. There is no design that you 'must' follow for the Receipts and Payments account and the Statement of Assets and Liabilities. You must give at least the minimum information required by law and the wider church. Obviously, it is best to present this in a consistent way from year to year. The example shown in this book gives a recommended design for the trustees' report and annual accounts.

This guidance aims to make annual reporting easier. By producing the recommended reports and accounts you will also have provided all the information required by law.

4.2 What do PCCs have to do to produce their annual report and accounts?

Summarise:

● What went into the bank, for what fund (purpose) and where it came from (receipts).

● What came out of the bank, from what fund and what was it spent on (payments).

● The year end bank balance(s) on all the funds of the PCC and particulars of any investments and other non-monetary assets as at the end of the year (even if sold since) and to what fund they belong.

- Details of any amounts owing to the PCC (e.g. Gift Aid and GASDS claims) and of any loans, unpaid bills or other liabilities of the PCC as at the end of the year (even if paid since) and to what fund they relate.

To do this:

Consider how money is received and spent by the PCC and then decide on the most sensible account headings to use in order to complete the annual Return of Parish Finance. The return has two main sections: incoming resources and resources expended and these are divided into categories and account headings to give more detail.

Some basic practical and consistent account headings have been identified for the PCC to adopt or use as a checklist. They relate to parish life and link easily to the Receipts and Payment reports and the annual Return of Parish Finance report.

The following examples use these account headings:

Receipt account headings	Payment account headings
Planned giving	Parish share
Collections at services	Mission giving and donations
Gift Aid recovered	Church running expenses
Receipts from church activities (e.g. fees for weddings and funerals)	Fundraising ctivities (e.g. costs of fetes and other events)

Example individual account descriptions are given in Chapter 2. The individual account descriptions included in each heading can be as detailed as the PCC wishes. Each time you get or spend money you also need to record the fund that you used. If you use a cashbook or spreadsheets you simply add extra columns for the funds. Church specific software will manage this for you.

Using the limited number of categories and account headings enables your accounts to be compared with other parishes. Doing this gives an overall picture of how parishes within each diocese or across the country are getting and spending their money.

The category groupings bring together similar account headings. For example, all donations are shown as voluntary receipts and the running costs of the church are shown as church activities. The headings given here are suggested for parish use, and are in line with guidance from the Charity Commission and the Return of Parish Finance.

There are two main sections to the accounts: 'Receipts' and 'Payments'. These are divided into categories and account headings to give more detail. Using the examples above, the receipts would be grouped together in categories:

Receipts categories for reporting	Receipt account headings
Voluntary receipts	Planned giving
	Collections at services
	Gift Aid recovered
Church activities	Receipts from church activities (e.g. fees for weddings and funerals)

Using the examples above, the payments would be grouped together in categories:

Payments categories for reporting	Payment accounts headings
Church Activities	Parish share
	Mission giving and donations
	Church running expenses
Costs of generating funds	Fundraising ctivities (e.g. costs of fetes and other events)

Once the account headings have been decided and the funds that the money belongs to have been identified, receipts and payments can be recorded.

4.3 Practical hints and tips

1. The PCC must record full particulars of any significant gifts in kind in the accounting records, so that those that the PCC still owns at the year end can be listed as 'non-monetary' assets in the Statement of Assets and Liabilities. Depreciation does not need to be recorded, as it doesn't feature in Receipts and Payments accounting.

2. **Recording money the PCC receives or pays that covers more than one account heading:**

   For example, the PCC may be given money or make payments that cover more than one account heading, such as purchasing Bibles partly for the bookstall and partly as a gift in kind to a missionary society.

   The PCC needs to divide the money between the different activity account headings – it is called **apportionment** and should be done on a 'reasonable basis'. This means that if 20% of the Bibles were for the bookstall and 80% for the mission, then 20% of the cost would be shown as bookstall costs and 80% as mission grants.

3. **Recording money the PCC receives or pays that covers more than one fund:**

   The PCC may receive or pay out money that relates to more than one fund. For example, building work that is partly normal maintenance out of the general fund and partly improvement. The latter may have to come out of a restricted fund for the building. In such a situation, it should be split on a reasonable basis, e.g. if the building work done is 50% normal maintenance and 50% improvement, then the payment will be split half to the general fund and half to the restricted fund.

4. **Netting off is not allowed:**

   The PCC must record all receipts and payments gross, so for example if the PCC has a fete which costs £100 for materials/publicity and it raises £500 from the fete, then the accounts must not show the receipts less the payments which would be an overall receipt of £400. In this case the PCC must show:

   i. Receipts = £500

   ii. Payments = £100

Where money simply passes through the PCC's bank account, but the funds do not belong to the PCC, then the receipt and the payment should not be included in the PCC's annual Receipts and Payments account. This is because the PCC was only the agent or conduit for the money recorded.

4.4 Trustees' Annual Report (TAR)

This report gives the PCC the chance to tell everyone the aims of the church and what the PCC is doing to make them happen. The PCC can share 'good news' stories and how people's giving made them possible.

Trustees are collectively responsible for this report, and the drafting should not just be left to the treasurer. Its aim is to give a clear and concise description of the mission and ministry of the church. Also remember that this report is meant for anyone, so that they understand why and how the church works.

The preparation of the Trustees' Annual Report is covered in Chapter 3. An example of the Trustees' Annual Report is shown in Chapter 5.

4.5 Receipts and Payments account

The first financial report shows how the parish's cash was received and spent and how this related to your funds. You can produce a receipt and payment summary for:

a. each fund – summarising all of the cash going in to or out of each fund separately;

b. each type of fund – summarising all of the cash going in to or out of each fund type separately;

c. all three types of fund combined in a single statement with each type in a separate column.

The recommended option is **option C**. However, certain information is needed to complete the receipts and payments summary. The following table shows you the questions you need to answer and where the information is put on the report.

Section on the account	What question is being asked by the section:
Receipts	What cash did the PCC receive? This will include under 'other receipts' the money you got (if any) from selling any asset (such as a building or land) or investments.
Payments	What cash did the PCC spend – and on what? This will include under 'Other payments' any money you converted into other valuable assets (such as buying a building or land) or investments.
Excess of receipts (or payments)	Were the PCC's receipts more or less than its payments? In other words, did the PCC's cash assets increase or decrease?
Bank balance at beginning of year	How much was in the bank when the PCC started the year?
Transfers	How much money did the PCC move between different funds?
Bank balance at end of year	How much was in the bank when the PCC ended the year?
Last year's totals for comparison. (Although this is not legally required, it is strongly recommended to help the reader better understand the accounts.)	Was this year better or worse than last year and in what way?
All amounts should to be rounded to the nearest £	**Remember there is no netting off. Expenses and costs must be shown in full.**

The St Emillion's report and accounts demonstrates how this works in practice:

4.6 Statement of Assets and Liabilities

This report shows the total financial resources of the parish and how they are allocated to funds. The following table shows what information to include in each section:

Statement of Assets and Liabilities	
Section of the statement	**What question is being asked by the section:**
Cash	How much money is in the bank/petty cash accounts at the end of the year? The amount shown on the Receipts and Payments account.
Other monetary assets	What other money does the PCC have or is owed to it? This includes such items as: ● Gift Aid claimed but not yet received ● Loans made by the parish ● Money owed for services or work provided by the parish ● Legacies where entitlement is proved, but the money (or other asset) has not yet been received.
Investments assets	What investments does the PCC have? This includes investment securities as well as bank/term deposits and also property or land that brings income to the parish or increases in value. The amount shown is either the deposit balance or the amount paid for the investment.
Assets retained for church use	What other assets of this kind does the PCC have, e.g. land, houses, cars, computers, printers etc.? If the PCC doesn't know the cost and acquisition date, it can just describe these assets and how long they have been in the ownership of the PCC. The PCC doesn't have to value them nor show an estimated or insurance value.
Liabilities	What amounts did the PCC owe at the end of the year? This includes such items as: ● Amount of any loans to the PCC still to be paid back ● Payroll deductions and employer contributions relating to the financial year that are unpaid at the end of the year ● Only money actually owed at the year end (or the best estimate of it) should be included.
	All amounts should to be rounded to the nearest £.

When deciding what needs to be shown as an asset or liability, the PCC needs to ask itself: Is it vital information? This means that if the PCC left that information out, would it make the financial position harder to understand?

For example, at the end of the year the PCC owed a builder £5 for wood – this amount will not make a big difference to the church so need not be shown. The independent examiner can give advice if the PCC is not sure.

Although the PCC is putting a lot of information into these accounts there are often things that it wants to explain or add. For example, it may need to explain what its funds are given for or any transfers between funds that were made. Or where it doesn't know the end of year open market value of an asset that isn't a sum of money (e.g. a lease on a building; stocks and shares; a bequest of such assets) it can just give identifying information about the asset, its condition and use, also its cost (if purchased). The PCC can do all this by adding 'notes' to the accounts.

Notes to the accounts may help the reader to understand the accounts better. For example, the PCC might choose to include further details about payments and receipts, e.g. a breakdown of church running costs. There is a balance to be struck between providing useful additional information to the reader, and providing so much detail that it can confuse rather than help. These notes can be written as part of the Statement of Assets and Liabilities or else within the Trustees' Annual Report. This is illustrated in the St Emillion's reports.

4.7 Independent examiner's report

Who checks the PCC's accounts?

The PCC needs to show that its accounts comply with the Charities Act.

At the end of the year the PCC must have the accounts checked by an independent person who is not on the PCC (or any PCC sub-committee) and who understands charity accounting (this applies to all PCCs under Church regulations). The independent examiner will need to examine the accounts and underlying records within the context of the annual report, and provide the PCC with a statutory form of report on the accounts.

Chapter 1 provides guidance on recruiting an independent examiner, and working with them.

4.8 What happens next?

The PCC then needs to approve the Trustees' Annual Report, with the accounts and Independent Examiner's Report attached. Note, the accounts are the responsibility of the whole PCC and not just the treasurer. Then the Report and Accounts are ready for a wider audience.

4.9 Who does the PCC give the report and accounts to?

The accounts are published – put on notice boards within the church at least seven days before the Annual Parochial Church Meeting. The PCC treasurer will normally be required to explain the accounts to the meeting. Copies of these reports are sent to the Diocesan Office with the Parish Return of Finance report.

The accounts are public documents, so every member of the public has a right to see them and can request a copy.

If the PCC has registered as a charity with the Charity Commission it must file a copy of its report and accounts and completed annual return. (This involves uploading a pdf of the report and accounts completing the online report.)

4.10 End of year checklists:

Before sending the accounts to the independent examiner the PCC has to:

Question	Answer
Ensure that it has included all bank accounts and funds relevant to the PCC	The Receipts and Payments account(s) must include all receipts and payments that the PCC is responsible for. Examples might include youth funds, flower funds, coffee money, lunch clubs etc. that have separate bank or cash accounts.
Properly recorded all loose plate giving?	Normal Sunday collections have been recorded as part of the general fund. Collections made for special purposes have been recorded against the relevant fund(s).
Recorded any money paid out as cash from Sunday collections?	All money collected should normally be banked gross. If a small payment has been made out of cash, this should be recorded as a petty cash receipt and then as a petty cash payment, with evidence of what the money was used for – shop receipt etc... (The relevant fund(s) must be recorded in each case.)
Recorded all standing orders?	Only standing orders that have been paid or received within the financial year should be recorded in that year.
Kept all Gift Aid records up to date?	This may be managed by a Gift Aid secretary.
Record the tax reclaimed on Gift Aid?	Any Gift Aid received on money for a specific fund must be allocated to that fund. The PCC may have sent its Gift Aid claim to the HMRC before the end of the year, but will only record the Gift Aid received in the bank during the year. The Statement of Assets and Liabilities will record any significant sums of Gift Aid claimed from HMRC, but not yet received.
Properly recorded endowment fund interest?	This has been recorded as income against the restricted fund the endowment relates to or to the general fund if there were no restrictions. It should not be recorded as income to the endowment funds.
Ensured all payments are properly evidenced?	Are all payments supported by receipts, invoices, expense claims or other paperwork?
Ensured any new designation of funds made by the PCC during the year have been recorded?	If the PCC has decided to designate any of its unrestricted funds during the year, this needs to be recorded.
Ensure that any non-monetary assets acquired by the PCC and any liabilities incurred by the PCC have been recorded in enough detail?	If payment has been made for the asset or the asset has been donated or bequeathed to the PCC, this information needs to be recorded. If the PCC has incurred a liability full details of it also need to be recorded.

chapter 5

Receipts and Payments Accounting Example

ANNUAL REPORT AND FINANCIAL STATEMENTS

For the year ended 31 December 2016

The Parochial Church Council of St Emillion's Church, Barchester

The Parochial Church Council of St Emillion's Church, Barchester

Example Trustees' Annual Report (Accruals accounting)

2016 Report and Accounts for the Parochial Church Council of St Emillion's Church, Barchester

Aims and purposes

St Emillion's Parochial Church Council (PCC) has the responsibility of cooperating with the incumbent, the Reverend Samuel Weller, in promoting in the ecclesiastical parish, the whole mission of the Church, pastoral, evangelistic, social and ecumenical. The PCC is also specifically responsible for the maintenance of the Church Centre complex of St Emillion's, The Green, Barchester.

Objectives and Activities

The PCC is committed to enabling as many people as possible to worship at our church and to become part of our parish community at St Emillion's. The PCC maintains an overview of worship throughout the parish and makes suggestions on how our services can involve the many groups that live within our parish. Our services and worship put faith into practice through prayer and Scripture, music and sacrament.

When planning our activities for the year, we have considered the Charity Commission's guidance on public benefit and, in particular, the supplementary guidance on charities for the advancement of religion.

In particular, we try to enable ordinary people to live out their faith as part of our parish community through:

● Worship and prayer; learning about the gospel; developing their knowledge and trust in Jesus.

● Provision of pastoral care for people living in the parish

● Missionary and outreach work.

To facilitate this work, it is important that we maintain the fabric of the church of St Emillion and the Church Centre complex.

Achievements and performance

Worship and prayer

The PCC is keen to offer a range of services during the week and over the course of the year that our community find both beneficial and spiritually fulfilling. For example, evening prayers provide a quiet, intimate and reflective environment for worship, while opportunities are provided for people to engage in more outgoing worship such as that provided by the youth group within our parish.

This year we have been successful in welcoming more families into our church and have agreed a new style of Family Worship on the morning of the third Sunday each month. This has meant that special arrangements have had to be made for baptisms and for welcoming the families at corporate worship on the 1st Sunday of each month. It is pleasing to be able to report that the new arrangements have been well received since they came into operation during September. They will be reviewed by the PCC after 12 months. In addition, a great deal of time and thought was spent during the year on making best use of the new services. Many have said how much easier it is to follow the services now that they are printed out in booklets.

All are welcome to attend our regular services. At present there are 173 parishioners on the church electoral roll, 91 of whom are not resident within the parish. Eighteen names were added during the year and nine were removed either through death or because they moved away from the parish. The average weekly attendance, counted during October, was 107, but this number increased at festivals, and two Christmas carol services had to be held to seat all those who wished to attend.

As well as our regular services, we enable our community to celebrate and thank God at the milestones of the journey through life. Through baptism we thank God for the gift of life; in marriage, public vows are exchanged with God's blessing; through funeral services friends and family express their grief and give thanks for the life that is now complete in this world, and commend the person into God's keeping.

Deanery Synod

Three members of the PCC sit on the Deanery Synod. This provides the PCC with an important link between the parish and the wider structures of the Church. This year the PCC has also focused its attention on the questions posed to parishes in the deanery about the most effective deployment of stipendiary and non-stipendiary clergy.

The Church Centre complex

We want our church to be open to our community for private prayer. Unfortunately, since the theft of valuable church artefacts from St Augustus' Church, in the neighbouring parish, we have felt unable to leave the church open at all times for private worship. We are, however, pleased that a rota of parishioners has enabled us to open the church at weekends and for all public holidays in the past year.

The state of the nave roof has been causing concern for some time. After many years, during which routine maintenance has been carried out, a detailed report on its condition will be prepared by the architect at the next routine inspection in April 2017. We have already anticipated the need for major structural renewal, and it is our policy to make provisions from general income in the hope that an urgent appeal can be avoided.

The kitchen in the church hall was refurbished during August and the new environment meets the stringent health and safety requirements and allows us to continue the old people's luncheon club on Saturdays. Eighteen people regularly attend at our luncheon club, twelve of whom are parishioners. We were particularly pleased to be able to extend the services of our club to the members of the Barchester Green Methodist Chapel luncheon club when the death of Alice Luther, the main organiser of that club, forced its closure.

During the week the hall is used by our mothers and toddlers group on Wednesdays. Fifteen children and their carers have been regular attenders at the group. During the summer the group organised two outings including older siblings during the school holidays. In July, 20 children and their parents went for the day to Longleat and later in the holidays we had the hottest day of the year for our family outing to New Milton.

The crèche runs in the hall on Tuesday and Thursday mornings. There are 12 regular attenders at the crèche, which is organised by Sally Pincent, the council's peripatetic childcare co-ordinator who runs crèches at our church as well as at St Augustus' on Mondays and Wednesdays. She has a rota of volunteers from the parish who help her, all of whom have been CRB checked. The crèche had an OFSTED inspection during the year and passed with flying colours.

Pastoral care

Some members of our parish are unable to attend church due to sickness or age. Reverend Samuel Weller has visited all church members who have requested it, to celebrate communion with them either at their homes or in hospital. Miss Finching has continued to organise a rota of volunteers to visit all who are sick or unable to get out for any other reason, to keep them in touch with church life.

Mission and evangelism

Helping those in need is a demonstration of our faith. The Mission and Evangelism Committee is to be congratulated on its fundraising efforts. £1,350 was raised for the Southern Africa Famine appeal. It is good that these efforts on behalf of others can be combined with opportunities for fellowship.

Our parish magazine is distributed quarterly to all parishioners on the church electoral roll and is available at the church hall. The magazine keeps our parishioners informed of the important matters affecting our church and articles that help develop our knowledge and trust in Jesus.

Ecumenical relationships

The church is a member of Churches Together in Barchester and of the Salisbury Interfaith Forum. We have held joint services on the fourth Sunday of every month with the Barchester Green Methodist Church, and for the first time this year have joined with them both for our Lent courses and to run an Alpha course in the autumn. The Alpha course has led a number of people to attend other church activities and services. We have also worked with Barchester Green Methodist Church and Millfield Baptist Church to deliver a flyer to every home in the town advertising the Christmas services of all three churches.

Financial review

Total receipts on unrestricted funds were £64,200, of which £42,000 was unrestricted voluntary donations, and a further £8,700 was from Gift Aid. Restricted donations of £5,800 were also received and are detailed in the financial statements. The freehold house at 36 Church Street continues to be let temporarily, which provided a gross income of £3,700.

The planned giving through envelopes and banker's orders increased by 8% and it was good to see that the use of Gift Aid envelopes increased. Total income, including tax recovered but excluding the legacy, went up by only 3% compared with last year. This was partly due to the Christmas Bazaar not being held this year. We were grateful for a pecuniary legacy of £1,000 from the estate of Mrs Mary Rudge. £2,000 was set aside towards the cost of the much needed cleaning of the organ. The work was completed in time for Christmas.

£61,350 was spent from unrestricted funds to provide the Christian ministry from St Emillion's Church, including the contribution to the diocesan parish share that increased by 12% in the year and largely provides the stipends and housing for the clergy.

The sum that the churches in the deanery have to find is shared between the churches according to a formula that is based mainly on a head count of the congregations. We have to find more of the sum at St Emillion's, as the size of our congregation increased more compared with other churches.

The net result for the year was an excess of receipts over payments of £2,750 on unrestricted funds. Adding bank and deposit balances brought forward at the beginning of the year, the balances carried forward at 31 December on unrestricted funds totalled £10,350, of which £5,300 has been set aside to meet the costs of cleaning and maintaining the church organ and is carried forward as a designated fund.

Reserves policy

It is PCC policy to try to maintain a balance on unrestricted funds that equates to at least three months' unrestricted payments. This is equivalent to £15,000. It is held to smooth out fluctuations in cash flow and to meet emergencies. The cash balance of £10,350 held on unrestricted (including designated) funds at the year end, together with the amounts payable to and by the PCC, was less than half of this target. It is the PCC's hope to increase this over time, as and when investment income recovers.

The balance of £17,050 in the fabric restricted fund is retained towards meeting the cost of the nave roof repairs detailed above. It is our policy to invest £5,000 of our fund balances with the CCLA Church of England Deposit Fund, and the remainder in the CCLA Church of England Investment Fund.

Optional information

Volunteers

We would like to thank all the volunteers who work so hard to make our church the lively and vibrant community it is. In particular, we want to mention our churchwardens Mrs Allen and Mr Tapley, who have worked so tirelessly on our behalf, and Mrs Neckett, who has helped us all to understand the church's accounts and its finances.

Structure, governance and management

The Parochial Church Council is a corporate body established by the Church of England. The PCC operates under the Parochial Church Council Powers Measure.

The method of appointment of PCC members is set out in the Church Representation Rules. At St Emillion's the membership of the PCC consists of the incumbent (our vicar), churchwardens, the reader and members elected by those members of the congregation who are on the electoral roll of the church.

The PCC members are responsible for making decisions on all matters of general concern and importance to the parish, including deciding on how the funds of the PCC are to be spent. New members receive initial training into the workings of the PCC.

The full PCC met six times during the year with an average level of attendance of 80%. Given its wide responsibilities the PCC has a number of committees each dealing with a particular aspect of parish life.

These committees, which include worship, mission and outreach and fabric and finance, are all responsible to the PCC and report back to it regularly, minutes of their decisions being received by the full PCC and discussed as necessary.

Administrative information

St Emillion's Church is situated in The Green, Barchester. It is part of the Diocese of Salisbury within the Church of England. The correspondence address is The Vicarage, Church Street, Barchester. The PCC is a body corporate (PCC Powers Measure 1956, Church Representation Rules 2011) and a charity currently excepted from registration with the Charity Commission.

PCC members who have served at any time from 1 January 2016 until the date this report was approved are:

Ex officio members:

- Incumbent: The Reverend Samuel Weller (chair)

- Reader: Mr Robert Sawyer

- Warden: Mrs Arabella Allen

- Warden: Mr Mark Tapley

Elected members:

- Mr Frederick Trent, representative on Deanery Synod

- Mr Peter Magnus Secretary, representative on Deanery Synod

- Mr John Fielding, representative on Deanery Synod

- Miss Flora Finching (from 5 April 2016)

- Mrs Charlotte Neckett, treasurer

- Mr George Radfoot

- Miss Edith Granger

- Mrs Tilly Slowboy (vice-chair)

- Miss Emily Wardle (until 5 April 2016)

- Mr Mark Walker

- Miss Emma Haredale

- Mr Julius Handford (until 5 April 2016)

- Miss Elizabeth Hexham

- Mr Ralph Nickleby (from 5 April 2016)

Approved by the PCC on 8 March 2017 and signed on their behalf by the Reverend Samuel Weller (PCC chairman)

Independent Examiner's Report to the Trustees of St Emilion's Parochial Church Council

I report on the accounts of the church for the year ended 31 December 2016 which are set out on pages xx to xx.

Respective Responsibilities of Trustees and Examiner

The church's trustees are responsible for the preparation of the accounts. The church's trustees consider that an audit is not required for this year under section 144(2) of the Charities Act 2011 (the 2011 Act)) and that an independent examination is needed.

It is my responsibility to:

- Examine the accounts (under section 145 of the 2011 Act);

- To follow the procedures laid down in the General Directions given by the Charity Commissioners (under section 145(5)(b) of the 2011 Act); and

- To state whether particular matters have come to my attention.

Basis of Independent Examiner's report

My examination was carried out in accordance with the general Directions given by the Charity Commission. An examination includes a review of the accounting records kept by the charity and a comparison of the accounts presented with those records. It also includes consideration of any unusual items or disclosures in the accounts, and seeking explanations from you as trustees concerning any such matters. The procedures undertaken do not provide all the evidence that would be required in an audit and consequently no opinion is given as to whether the accounts present a 'true and fair view' and the report is limited to those matters set out in the statement below.

Independent examiner's statement

In connection with my examination, no matter has come to my attention:

1.   which gives me reasonable cause to believe that in any material respect the requirements

- to keep accounting records in accordance with section 130 of the 2011 Act; and

- to prepare accounts which accord with the accounting records and comply with the accounting requirements of the 2011 Act have not been met; or

2.   to which, in my opinion, attention should be drawn in order to enable a proper understanding of the accounts to be reached.

(Name) (Date)

(Relevant professional qualification or body)

(Address)

Receipts and Payments Accounts

PAROCHIAL CHURCH COUNCIL OF ST EMILLION'S CHURCH, BARCHESTER

Financial Statements for the Year Ended 31 December 2016

Receipts and Payments Accounts

	Note	Unrestricted funds £	Restricted funds £	Endowment funds £	TOTAL 2016 £	TOTAL 2015 £
RECEIPTS						
Voluntary receipts:						
Planned giving		29,400	–	–	29,400	27,200
Collections at services		9,900	–	–	9,900	10,600
All other giving/voluntary receipts	5a	2,700	5,800	–	8,500	7,050
Gift Aid recovered		8,700	–	–	8,700	8,300
		50,700	5,800	–	56,500	53,150
Activities for generating funds	5b	3,500	–	–	3,500	4,250
Investment income	5c	4,600	950	–	5,550	5,300
Church activities	5d	5,400	–	–	5,400	5,150
Total receipts		64,200	6,750	–	70,950	67,850
PAYMENTS						
Church activities:						
Diocesan parish contribution		41,500	–	–	41,500	37,050
Clergy and staffing costs		1,900	–	–	1,900	1,800
Church running expenses	5e	13,700	1,850	–	15,550	15,250
Hall running costs		1,200	–	–	1,200	1,200
Mission giving and donations	5f	2,550	1,350	–	3,900	2,550
		60,850	3,200	–	64,050	57,850
Costs of generating funds		500	–	–	500	500
Total payments		61,350	3,200	–	64,550	58,350
Excess of receipts over payments		2,850	3,550	–	6,400	9,500
Transfers between funds	4	(100)	100	–	–	–
		2,750	3,650	–	6,400	9,500
Cash at bank and in hand at 1 January		7,600	13,400	–	21,000	11,500
Cash at bank and in hand at 31 December		10,350	17,050	–	27,400	21,000

Statement of Assets and Liabilities

	Note	Unrestricted funds	Restricted funds	Endowment funds	TOTAL 2016	TOTAL 2015
		£	£	£	£	£
Cash funds						
Bank current account		300	–	–	300	350
Deposit funds		10,050	17,050		27,100	20,650
		10,350	17,050	–	27,400	21,000
Other monetary assets						
Gift Aid recoverable		2,240	–	–	2,240	–
Investment assets						
Investment fund shares at market value	3	–	–	20,000	20,000	19,500
Assets retained for church use	2	59,000	–	–	59,000	59,000
Liabilities						
Organ cleaning/tune		6,200	–	–	6,200	–

Notes

1. The financial statements of the PCC have been prepared in accordance with the Church Accounting Regulations 2006 using the Receipts and Payments basis

2. Fixed assets retained for church use is the freehold house at 36 Church Street, purchased 5 November 1984, at cost.

3. The endowment fund, a donation in 1999 by R. H.Smith, has to be retained as a capital fund, but the income is for ordinary church purposes. It is invested in CCLA Church of England Investment Fund shares.

4. The movements in designated and restricted funds during the year were:

	Bal b/fwd	Receipts	Payments	Transfer	Bal c/fwd
Designated					
Organ fund	3,300	–	–	2,000	5,300
Restricted					
Church fabric (inc tower)	13,400	5,050	1,400	–	17,050
Southern Africa Famine Appeal	–	1,350	1,350	–	–
Flower fund	–	350	450	100	–
	13,400	6,750	3,200	100	17,050

The transfer to the organ fund was from ordinary unrestricted funds to meet the balance of the cleaning/tuning costs.

The fabric fund represents accumulated donations and appeals for fabric maintenance, which can only be spent for that purpose.

The Southern Africa Famine appeal represents funds raised by the Mission and Evangelism Committee to relieve poverty and hardship in the recent famine in Southern Africa.

The flower fund represents a donation from a parishioner to be spent on Easter lilies in memory of her recently deceased mother.

The cost of the flowers is included in costs of services. A further £100 was designated from the general fund to meet the full cost of lilies.

5. Further Analysis of Receipts and Payments Accounts

	Note	Unrestricted funds £	Restricted funds £	Endowment funds £	TOTAL 2016 £	TOTAL 2015 £
Receipts						
a) **All other giving/voluntary receipts**						
Donations		1,700	5,800	–	7,500	7,050
Legacy		1,000	–	–	1,000	–
		2,700	5,800	–	8,500	7,050
b) **Activities for generating funds:**						
Parish magazine – advertising		1,100	–	–	1,100	1,050
Summer fete and Christmas bazaar		2,400	–	–	2,400	2,500
Rummage sales		–	–	–	–	700
		3,500	–	–	3,500	4,250
c) **Investment income:**						
Dividends on CCLA Investment Funds		500	–	–	500	500
Bank and CCLA Deposit Fund interest		400	950	–	1,350	1,100
Rent – temporary let on curate's house		3,700	–	–	3,700	3,700
		4,600	950	–	5,550	5,300
d) **Church activities:**						
Fees for weddings and funerals		400	–	–	400	300
Parish magazine income – sales		1,100	–	–	1,100	1,050
Church Centre lettings – local community use		3,900	–	–	3,900	3,800
		5,400	–	–	5,400	5,150
Payments						
e) **Church running expenses:**						
Sunday school teacher training		1,000	–	–	1,000	–
Organ inspection		–	–	–	–	150
Costs of services		2,600	450	–	3,050	2,100
Printing and stationery		1,100	–	–	1,100	1,200
Church building running expenses		4,700	–	–	4,700	4,800
Parish magazine printing		1,800	–	–	1,800	1,800
Church repairs and maintenance		2,500	1,400	–	3,900	5,200
		13,700	1,850	–	15,550	15,250
f) **Mission giving and donations**						
CMS		1,200	–	–	1,200	1,200
Southern Africa Famine appeal		1,350	1,350	–	2,700	–
Earthquake appeal		–	–	–	–	1,350
		2,550	1,350	–	3,900	2,550

chapter 6

Accruals Accounting?

6.1 Accounts structure

The financial statements are a report in financial terms on the activities and resources of the charity, and must comprise:

- A Statement of Financial Activities (SOFA) for the year that shows all incoming resources made available to the PCC and all resources expended by it, and reconciles all movements in its funds. The statement should consist of a single set of accounting statements and be presented in columnar form where the PCC has restricted income or endowment funds.

- A balance sheet that shows the assets, liabilities and funds of the charity. SORP 2015 also comments that the balance sheet may be presented in columnar format. This is not mandatory but using it ensures a more detailed and therefore informative presentation of the required analysis of assets and liabilities by category of fund. The balance sheet (or the notes to the financial statements) should also explain in general terms how the funds may or, because of restrictions imposed by donors, must be utilised.

- Notes to the financial statements, explaining the accounting policies adopted and explaining or expanding upon the information contained in the accounting statements referred to above, or which provide further useful information. This will include notes analysing the figures in the primary financial statements and explaining the relationships between them.

- A cash flow statement. The largest PCCs with £500k gross income for the year must provide a cash flow statement under FRS 102. Such parishes, if exceeding £1m gross income, will require a full audit, and the PCC's auditor will advise accordingly.

The financial statements should include all the money and other assets entrusted to the PCC for whatever purpose, and show how they have been expended during the year and how the unexpended balance of each fund was held at the year end.

The corresponding figures for the previous year must be provided in the financial statements in accordance with generally accepted accounting practice, i.e. adjusted where necessary to show them on the same basis as the current year's figures.

However, under SORP (FRS 102), the corresponding figures for last year in respect of the SOFA's fund-accounting columns (and those of the balance sheet if that option is taken up) must now be shown – either on the face of the SOFA /Balance Sheet or else 'prominently' in the accounts notes. The latter option can easily be achieved for the SOFA by copying last year's SOFA into the accounts notes but omitting its comparative figures column – subject to any changes that may be needed for comparability.

6.2 The notes to the accounts and the principle of materiality

Information is material and therefore has relevance if its omission or misstatement could influence the economic decisions of users made on the basis of the financial statements. Transactions or amounts that are clearly insignificant need not be separately shown or explained in the financial statements. As a general rule, a transaction or amount may be treated as insignificant ('immaterial') if it is without doubt too trivial to influence the reader of the financial statements. Too much detail about small items may confuse the overall picture, but if there is doubt about whether or not something is 'material', the information should be included. The exception to this is related party transactions, which are by definition all material.

6.3 Accounting policies

In order to understand the figures in the financial statements, the reader needs to know the basis on which they have been prepared. The 'accounting policies' note to the financial statements should therefore disclose that the financial statements are prepared under the current Church Accounting Regulations and comply with the current Charities SORP and applicable accounting standard FRS 102.

In addition, the significant accounting policies and assumptions adopted for dealing with any material items should be briefly but clearly explained in the notes to the financial statements. They will include an explanation of the estimation techniques that have been used, where judgement is required to record the value of incoming or outgoing resources and of assets and liabilities.

The accounting policies adopted must comply with FRS 102 (in particular sections 2 and 10) and must also be consistent with the 'going concern' concept, namely that the PCC is considered to be a going concern for the foreseeable future (normally at least one year from the date of signing the Annual Report and accounts), and must provide relevant, reliable, comparable and understandable information.

A model set of accounting policies is set out below. PCCs should add to and amend these as appropriate for their particular circumstances.

The financial statements should be approved at a meeting of the PCC and the balance sheet signed on the PCC's behalf and the date of approval shown. Only one signature is needed; this is usually that of the chairman of the meeting. However, in the case of the Church of England, where the chairman of the meeting will normally be the minister, it is good practice for the financial statements also to be signed by one other member, normally the treasurer or churchwarden, to underline the joint responsibility of both the minister and members of the PCC.

Model set of accounting policies

PCCs should adapt these as necessary. The accounting policies should be disclosed in the financial statements to assist the reader, particularly in respect of material items.

Basis of preparation

The PCC is a public benefit entity within the meaning of FRS 102. The financial statements have been prepared under the Charities Act 2011 and in accordance with the Church Accounting Regulations 2006 governing the individual accounts of PCCs, and with the Regulations' 'true and fair view' provisions, together with FRS 102 (2016) as the applicable accounting standards and the 2016 version of the Statement of Recommended Practice, Accounting and Reporting by Charities (SORP (FRS 102)).

INCOMING RESOURCES

Recognition of incoming resources	These are included in the Statement of Financial Activities (SOFA) when: 1. the PCC becomes legally entitled to the benefit of use of the resources; 2. and inflow of economic benefit is probable; 3. the monetary value can be measured with sufficient reliability.
Fundraising costs	Funds raised from events and trading activities (e.g. a fete, a garden party or sales of books and magazines) are reported gross in the SOFA – i.e. before any related costs that may have been deducted from the gross proceeds.

Grants and donations	Grants and donations are included in the SOFA when any preconditions preventing their use by the PCC have been met. For collections and planned giving this is when the funds are received.
Gift Aid Tax claims etc. on cash donations	Gift Aid and other tax claims are included in the SOFA at the same time as the cash donations to which they relate.
Gifts in kind	Gifts in kind are accounted for at a reasonable estimate of their fair value at the time of gift, if feasible, or else at the amount actually realised from their disposal.
	Gifts in kind for sale to fund the PCC are included in the accounts at their estimated fair value at the date of gift, if feasible – or else recognised when sold by the charity.
	Gifts in kind for the PCC's own use are included in the SOFA as incoming resources at their fair value when receivable, and expensed as and when consumed in use. Gifts of fixed assets, if material, are included in the balance sheet at their fair value and expensed over the asset's useful economic life.
Donated services and facilities	These are included in income (and at the same time in resources expended) at the estimated fair value to the PCC of the service or facility received.
Volunteer help	The value of any voluntary help received is not included in the accounts but is described in the Trustees' Annual Report.
Rental income	Rental income from the letting of the church is recognised when the rental is due.
Investment income	This is included in the accounts when receivable.
Investment gains and losses	This includes any gain or loss on the sale of investments and any gain or loss resulting from revaluing investments to market value at the end of the year.

EXPENDITURE AND LIABILITIES

Liability recognition	Liabilities are recognised as soon as there is a legal or constructive obligation and settlement is probable and quantifiable.
Governance costs	Include costs of the preparation and examination of statutory accounts, the costs of trustee meetings and cost of any legal advice to trustees on governance or constitutional matters.
Grants payable without performance conditions	These are recognised in the accounts when a commitment has been made externally and there are no preconditions still to be met for entitlement to the grant that remain within the control of the PCC.
Support Costs (If allocated across more than one heading)	Support costs include central functions and have been allocated to activity cost categories on a basis consistent with the use of resources (see section 6.13 of this chapter).

ASSETS

Consecrated and benefice property	In so far as consecrated and benefice property of any kind is excluded from the statutory definition of 'charity' by Section 10(2) (a) and (c) of the Charities Act 2011, such assets are not capitalised in the financial statements.
Movable church furnishings	These are capitalised at cost and depreciated over their useful economic life other than where insufficient cost information is available. In this case the item is not capitalised, but all items are included in the church's inventory in any case.
Tangible fixed assets for use by charity	These are capitalised if they can be used for more than one year, and cost at least £1,000. They are valued at cost or else, for gifts in kind, at a reasonable estimate of their open market value on receipt. Depreciation is calculated to write off the capitalised cost of fixed assets less their currently anticipated residual fair value over their estimated useful lives as follows: • Land — Nil • Buildings* — Nil • Fixtures and Fittings — 20 years • Computers — 3 years • Motor vehicles — x years *No depreciation is provided on buildings, as the currently estimated residual value of the properties is not less than their carrying value and the remaining useful life of these assets currently exceeds 50 years, so that any depreciation charges would be immaterial. An impairment review is carried out at each year end and any resultant loss identified included in expenditure for the year.
Investments	Investments quoted on a recognised stock exchange or whose value derives from them (CIFs etc.) are valued at market value at the year end. Other investment assets are included at trustees' best estimate of market value.
Trading stocks	These are valued at the lower of cost (or gift value) or year end fair value.
Short-term deposits	Include cash held on deposit either with the CCLA Church of England Funds or at the bank.

FUNDS

Unrestricted funds	These represent the remaining income funds of the PCC that are available for spending on the general purposes of the PCC, including amounts designated by the PCC for fixed assets for its own use or for spending on a future project and that are therefore not included in its 'free reserves' as disclosed in the trustees' report.
Restricted funds	These are income funds that must be spent on restricted purposes and details of the funds held and restrictions provided are shown in the notes to the accounts.
Endowment funds	These are restricted funds that must be retained as trust capital either permanently or subject to a discretionary power to spend capital as income, and where the use of any income or other benefit derived from the capital may be restricted or unrestricted. Full details of all their restrictions are shown in the notes to the accounts.

In addition to the disclosure of accounting policies described in this chapter further disclosures not relating to the figures are required to support the information in the SOFA and balance sheet. These are detailed below.

6.4 Charitable commitments

An unfulfilled commitment to make a grant or other voluntary contribution (funding) to a third party will not normally be a legally binding obligation, but where a valid expectation was created in the mind of the other party as at 31 December, with no pre-conditions for entitlement not yet met, it should be recognised in full as a liability in the financial statements for the year.

Where a PCC has authorised expenditure out of its unrestricted funds without making any accruable commitment as above, the PCC may wish to designate unrestricted funds to represent this future expenditure commitment. Any such amounts should be shown separately as designated funds, and clearly explained in the notes to the financial statements. The notes should also explain why the PCC has set up such a fund.

Particulars of all material commitments must be disclosed in the notes, whether or not the expenditure has been charged in the financial statements. The note should show the amounts involved, when the commitments are likely to be met and the movements on commitments previously reported.

Where later events make the recognition of liability no longer appropriate, the provision should be cancelled by credit against the relevant expenditure heading in the SOFA. The credit should mirror the treatment originally used to recognise the liability and should be disclosed separately, with a clear explanation in the notes to the financial statements, if material.

Disclosure and/or provision as appropriate may need to be made similarly for any commitment the PCC may have in relation to the repair and maintenance of capitalised or non-capitalised fixed assets such as benefice or consecrated property. If these amount to legal or constructive obligations, they will have to be accounted for as liabilities and charged to the SOFA. However, if there is no accruable liability contractual commitment at the balance sheet date, any funds set aside for repair and maintenance should be regarded as designated funds and not charged to the SOFA but instead should be disclosed as above as either contingent liabilities or cyclical maintenance commitments. The Annual Report should in any case say when the last quinquennial inspection was held and give details of the immediate works needed or needing completion.

6.5 Other commitments

Particulars of all other material binding commitments should also be disclosed. This may include, for example, operating leases for equipment or premises used by the church. Under FRS 102, the disclosure required here, for lessors and lessees alike, is the amount of the minimum payment commitment under operating leases up to the earliest break clause therein.

6.6 Loan liabilities secured on the PCC's assets

If any specific assets (whether land or other property) of the PCC are subject to a mortgage or charge, given as security for a loan or other liability, a note to the financial statements must disclose (a) particulars of those and (b) their carrying value.

6.7 Contingent liabilities

A contingency existing at the year end which is 'probable', i.e. considered likely to crystallise into a material liability, ceases to be 'contingent' for accounting purposes and should instead be accrued in the financial statements. The same applies to a previously unquantifiable present obligation that can now be quantified. The amount of the liability to be accrued must be capable of being reliably estimated with reasonable accuracy at the date on which the financial statements are approved.

The notes must disclose the nature of each contingency unless its possibility is 'remote', the uncertainties that are expected to affect the outcome and an estimate of the financial effect where practicable. The SORP says: 'in extremely rare cases where FRS 102 allows non-disclosure of information that would be expected to seriously prejudice the position of the [PCC] in a dispute with other parties, the general nature of the dispute and the reason why disclosure has note been made must be given'.

If such an estimate cannot be made, the financial statements should show why it is not practicable to make such an estimate.

6.8 Grants payable

If a PCC makes grants to institutions that are material in the context of its grant making, the PCC should disclose details of a sufficient number of these grants to provide an understanding of what the PCC has supported. The information given should include not only the purpose (or class of purpose), but also (subject to the exceptions, mentioned below), the name of the institution and total value of grants given.

The Trustees' Annual Report should include the PCC's policy for making grants and show the nature of the institution receiving them.

There is no requirement to disclose any grants if they are not material in relation to the PCC's total expenditure, but PCCs will usually wish to disclose all their major contributions to other charitable bodies, whatever their value, and this is to be encouraged. These can be shown in the Annual Report or in the notes to the financial statements or alternatively on the PCC's website if a link is provided in the accounts notes. Very exceptionally the disclosure of details of grants made to institutions could seriously prejudice the purposes of either the PCC or the recipient. The SORP's module 16.22–24 paragraphs explain what to do in these circumstances, by saying so in the notes and by disclosing their total number, value and general nature and that an exemption applies. The previous version of the SORP also required giving the sensitive information to the Charity Commission on a confidential basis – but this is not mentioned in the new SORP.

An unconditional or 'blanket' exception in s.132 of the Act provides that no disclosure need be made of the amount or the name of the recipient of any individual grant made out of a trust fund during the lifetime of its founder or spouse or civil partner. The only disclosures then required in the accounts notes are of the total amount of all such grants made in the year out of that trust fund and of their purpose(s).

6.9 Transactions with members of the PCC and other 'related parties'

Where a PCC enters into any material transaction, contract or other arrangement (including a grant or donation) with any 'related party', the amounts involved and the terms and conditions should be disclosed in the notes to the financial statements. Certain transactions need not be disclosed.

These include donations of any money or in kind from PCC members or those closely connected with them or any other 'related party' of the PCC (as long as any terms of trust imposed cannot be seen as altering materially the way the PCC operates), benefice property maintenance and employee contracts. These are unlikely to influence the separate independent interests of the charity. The total remuneration of employees is disclosed separately.

Any decision by the PCC to enter into a transaction should be, and should be seen to be, influenced only by the consideration of the PCC's own interests as a charity. This is reinforced by charity law rules which, in certain circumstances, can invalidate transactions where the PCC has a conflict of interest. Therefore, *all* transactions with related parties (including especially PCC members, their close family members and any legal entities under their control or significant influence) are to be disclosed. Transparency is particularly important where the relationship between the PCC and the related party suggests that the transaction could possibly have been influenced by interests other than the PCC's. It is possible, subject to charity law constraints, that the reported financial position and results may have been unlawfully affected by such transactions and to show that this has not happened information about these transactions and their propriety is therefore necessary for readers of the PCC's financial statements.

Transactions with PCC members personally or persons with a close family or business connection with them or with any other related party of the PCC are always regarded as material under SORP (FRS 102) and the amounts involved must therefore be disclosed, together with the following details required by the SORP:

● the ... relationship* [with the PCC and] the interest of the related party ... in the transaction;

● a description of the transaction(s);

● [any] outstanding balances ... at the [year end] and any provisions for doubtful debts;

● any amounts written off from such balances during the [year];

● the terms and conditions, including any security and the nature of the consideration to be provided in settlement;

● details of any guarantees given or received;

● any other elements of the transactions which are necessary for the understanding of the accounts.

(*related parties other than PCC members and their close family/business connections – see below – can be grouped together for an aggregate disclosure by type of transaction, e.g. for group members)

The name of the PCC member (if any) involved must be separately disclosed in the notes. Any 'private benefit' to a PCC member or close family/business connection must be separately disclosed together with the legal authority for such benefit. This includes details of the total salary costs where a PCC member is also a PCC employee. In such cases, the SORP requires disclosure of:

● the legal authority under which the payment was made ...;

● the name of the remunerated trustee;

● details of why the remuneration or other employment benefits were paid;

● the amount of remuneration paid;

● the amount of any pension contributions paid by the charity for the [year];

● the amount of any other benefit, for example any termination benefits, private health cover or the provision of a vehicle.

Where the PCC members have received no such remuneration or other taxable benefits, this fact must be stated.

Where travelling, subsistence or any other out-of-pocket expenses have been reimbursed to a member of the PCC or paid to a third party on a member's behalf, the aggregate amount of all such trustee-expenses must be disclosed in a note to the financial statements. The note must also indicate the nature of these personal expenses (e.g. travel, subsistence, entertainment etc.) and for how many of the PCC's members.

Where the PCC members have received no such reimbursement, this fact should be stated.

Sometimes PCC members act as agents for the PCC and make approved purchases on its behalf and are reimbursed for this expenditure, e.g. payment for stationery or candles. Such reimbursed expenditure is not personal to the trustee concerned, nor does it count as goods or services provided by a PCC member personally, and as it is not a personal expense there is no need to disclose it. Likewise, although no longer mentioned in the SORP, there is no need to disclose routine expenditure that is attributable collectively to the services provided by the PCC, such as providing reasonable refreshment for everyone at a PCC meeting.

Please note that in respect of related-party transactions all are now regarded as material. A transaction involving a PCC member or other related party must always be regarded as material regardless of its size. For this purpose, the SORP's glossary widens its definition of a 'related party' of the reporting charity by including a donor of land at any time, but no longer includes (i) a seconded employee's employer if not already a related party and likewise (ii) any non-charitable trust from which a trustee could benefit. FRS 102 requires disclosure of the total of all donations made to the PCC by related parties, trustees included. That would include any trustee-expense claims waived, this being just another class of gift in kind, unless immaterial, regardless of whether any individual related-party transactions have to be disclosed.

6.10 Staff costs and employee benefits

The total staff costs showing the split between gross wages and salaries, social security costs and pension costs, must be disclosed in the notes to the financial statements. (Clergy paid through the diocese are not PCC employees.)

The pension costs must be split between the employer costs of Defined Contribution schemes and the operating costs (other than finance costs) of Defined Benefit schemes and the total cost of any other forms of employee benefit must be shown separately, as must also the total of any staff redundancy or termination costs for the year.

Any costs of staff whose employment contracts are with a related party must be included.

All PCCs must disclose the average number of employees for the year. The employee numbers must be the average headcount, but full-time equivalents can be shown as well, as can staff deployment by activity type. Regardless of charity size or classification of expenditure in the SOFA, the numbers of employees of the PCC with 'total emoluments (excluding employer pension costs)' in each £10k bracket from £60k upwards must also be disclosed or else the fact there were none must be stated.

All PCCs must disclose the total cost of any 'employee benefits' received by trustees and 'key management personnel' for their services to the PCC. This is not optional for 'smaller' PCCs. Consideration needs to be given to identifying the 'key management personnel' who are required to report back directly or indirectly to the trustees in respect of any delegated decision-making powers, e.g. on the day-to-day management of the PCC.

6.11 Auditor's or independent examiner's remuneration

The notes to the financial statements should disclose separately the amount payable to the auditor or independent examiner in respect of:

- audit or independent examination services;

- other assurance services (if any) and other financial services such as taxation advice, consultancy, financial advice and accountancy, disclosing the fees separately under each head.

6.12 *Ex gratia* payments

The total amount or value of any:

- payment made;

- non-monetary benefit given;

- other expenditure of any kind;

- waiver of rights to property to which a PCC is entitled

which is made not as an application of funds or property for the general purposes of the PCC but in fulfilment of a compelling moral obligation, e.g. voluntarily surrendering part of a legacy if the reasonable needs of the testator's close family were not adequately provided for, should be disclosed in the notes to the financial statements, together with the 'legal authority or reason for making it'. It should be noted that special authorisation is needed for any proposed '*ex gratia* payment' and that it requires prior application to the Charity Commission, but that this does not normally include staff benefits of any kind.

6.13 Support costs

For the vast majority of PCCs, support costs will be for church running expenses and there will be no need to allocate them across different expenditure categories. For larger PCCs, however, support costs must be allocated to the relevant activity cost categories they support, as identified in the Trustees' Annual Report for performance reporting against the objectives set for the year.

Support costs now include governance costs (which are no longer disclosable on the face of the SOFA) and are costs incurred in the course of undertaking an activity that, while necessary, does not itself produce or constitute the output of the charitable activity. Similarly, costs will be incurred in supporting income-generating activities such as fundraising. They include generic costs such as payroll administration, accounting costs and computer maintenance as well as charity governance costs. Since they do not constitute an activity but instead enable activities to be undertaken, they are allocated to the relevant activity cost category they support according to the following principles:

● Where appropriate expenditure should be allocated directly to an activity cost category

● Items of expenditure that contribute directly to more than one activity cost category should be apportioned on a reasonable, justifiable and consistent basis, e.g. the cost of a staff member whose time is divided between a fundraising activity and a charitable activity should be apportioned on the basis of time spent on the particular activities.

There are a number of bases for apportionment that may be applied. Examples include:

● usage, e.g. electricity costs for the church and the hall

● per capita

● floor area

● time.

There should be a note to the financial statements that provides details of the total support costs incurred. If there are material items or categories of expenditure within this total, these should be separately identified. It is recommended that a grid is used that lists the activities and the separately identifiable material support costs that have been allocated.

chapter 7

Financial Statements (Accruals Accounting)

7.1 Statement of Financial Activities (SOFA)

This section lists the various incoming and outgoing resources for which PCCs may be responsible, and collates them under the activity headings that are mandatory for PCCs that are over the audit threshold. The recommended categories are in accordance with the Receipts and Payments categories. In accruals accounts, gifts in kind must be recognised at a monetary value. In addition, the depreciation of fixed assets in use by the PCC must be recognised. Also, expenditure on activities is to be presented by reference to their purpose rather than the nature of the expense.

7.1.1 Format

The SOFA should summarise for the year all incoming resources of the PCC, both capital (endowment) and income, and all resources expended by it, analysed in accordance with their nature or by activity and across the different categories of funds. It should also reconcile all movements in the funds since the previous 31 December.

An example SOFA is shown below. The SOFA should be supported by notes. A full example, including notes summarising the movements in significant individual funds, is shown in Chapter 8.

SORP (FRS 102) requires 'larger' PCCs to analyse their incoming resources (income and endowments) and resources expended (expenditure) by activity according to the purpose of that activity. The SORP also provides that smaller charities may use any analysis of incoming and outgoing resources that may be best suited to their circumstances. SORP (FRS 102) has slightly changed some of the terminology, e.g. 'incoming resources' is now 'income and endowments', 'resources expended' is now 'expenditure'. Also, 'governance costs' are no longer a separate line in the SOFA but are subsumed within 'support costs' and separately stated only in the accounts notes, and so on.

This chapter sets out how PCCs can group their incoming resources and resources expended into the SORP's purpose-based categories, and it is recommended that PCCs should, as far as possible, follow this approved layout, as this has been designed to cover most of the PCC's activities and sources of funding. This layout will also provide the information needed to complete the annual Return of Parish Finance.

Within the two separate sections of 'income and endowments' and 'resources expended', the individual sub-headings may be changed in order to present a true and fair view of the PCC's activities.

7.1.2 Income and endowments

All incoming resources becoming available to the PCC during the year must be summarised in the SOFA, distinguishing between those belonging to its unrestricted funds, its restricted income funds and its endowment capital funds. These should be classified in accordance with the activity headings set out in this chapter, namely:

Voluntary income

Activities for generating funds investment income

Church activities

Other incoming resources.

These comprise the total incoming resources, but do not necessarily equate to the 'gross income' (see Chapter 1, sections 1.3 and 1.4).

In the notes to the financial statements, endowment fund incoming resources should be analysed between permanent endowment and expendable endowment.

The SOFA should enable the reader of the financial statements to gain an accurate appreciation of the principal elements of the incoming resources of the charity, but should not be excessively detailed. Supporting analyses should be provided in notes to the financial statements.

7.1.3 Expenditure

All resources expended should be included in the SOFA in the year in which they are incurred.

The resources expended section of the SOFA should distinguish between various types of expenditure in a way that is appropriate to the PCC's activities, and between fund types (with supplementary analysis of any individual major funds by way of note). For all PCCs reporting their expenditure on the activity basis, the minimum expected classifications to be adopted are namely:

Church activities

Costs of generating funds

Other resources expended.

7.1.4 Transfers between funds

Each column in the SOFA should be totalled to show the net incoming/outgoing resources before transfers. If the PCC has restricted income funds or endowment funds, or if designated funds are shown separately in the SOFA, any transfers between funds should be shown as a separate line. Material transfers between the different classes of funds should not be netted off, but should be shown gross, with supporting explanations in the notes. Transfers should, of course, net off to zero in the total column.

7.1.5 Reporting investment gains and losses

Each column should again be totalled to give 'Net income and incoming endowments before investment gains and losses'. All gains and losses on investment assets are shown on the following line. It is not necessary to split the investment gain between realised and unrealised categories.

7.1.6 Net income and incoming endowments for the year

Other recognised gains and losses relate to the revaluations of functional fixed assets. These gains or losses should be recorded as part of the fund in which the relevant asset is or was held.

Each column of the statement will then be totalled to show the net movement in funds of the PCC for the year as shown in the example (Chapter 8). Please note that no reference has been made to pensions, currency gains or losses or extraordinary items, and should PCCs have these items, they should be shown separately within this section.

7.1.7 Reconciliation of funds

To the net movement in funds for the year for each column should be added the total funds brought forward from the previous balance sheet, to show the amounts of the total funds carried forward as shown in the balance sheet at the year end.

7.1.8 Comparative figures

In the SOFA, corresponding amounts for the previous year are required (in either the SOFA or the Notes to the Accounts) for each item in the fund accounting – columns on each line. Compliance can most easily be achieved by including a copy of last year's SOFA (without its comparative figures column) as a prominent accounts note after making any adjustments needed to show them on the same basis as this year's SOFA figures.

Accounting for income and endowments

7.1.9 Recognition in the Statement of Financial Activities (SOFA)

Members of the PCC have a legal duty to take reasonable care that everything they are entrusted with is properly applied, which in the first place means safeguarding everything to which the PCC becomes entitled as soon as this entitlement becomes legally enforceable. This includes not only actual receipts of the year but also any money or other property – whatever its source or purpose – that could have been received if the PCC had exercised its legal right to take possession of it. It should be accounted for within income and endowments of the PCC for the year.

The value of all resources – both for income and endowment funds – accruing to the PCC should be recorded in the SOFA as soon as it is practicable to do so. In all cases incoming resources should be recognised as and when the following three accounting requirements are met:

- entitlement – normally arises when a particular resource is receivable or the PCC's right to it becomes legally enforceable (unless its utilisation by the PCC has been deferred by the donor);

- probability – when it is more likely than not that the PCC will benefit from the incoming resource;

- measurement – when the monetary value of the incoming resource can be measured with sufficient reliability.

7.1.10 Gifts in kind

Where material, these should be included within 'All other giving/donations' in the SOFA as follows:

- Assets given for use by the PCC, e.g. photocopier for use in the church office, should be recognised as incoming resources at their fair value at the date of gift (i.e. market value).

- Where a gift has been made in kind but on trust for conversion into cash and subsequent application by the PCC, the incoming resource should normally be recognised in the accounting period at its fair value at the date of gift (i.e. market value); but in certain cases this will not be practicable. In these cases the income should be included in the accounting period in which the gift is sold.

- In respect of donated services and facilities, the amount that should be recognised is the price that the PCC would have to pay for an alternative resource of equivalent service or facility.

The basis of any valuation should be disclosed, in any case, unless the item is immaterial. Where material, an adjustment should be made to the original valuation upon subsequent realisation of the gift.

7.1.11 Donated services and facilities

A PCC may receive assistance in the form of donated facilities, beneficial loan arrangements, donated services (such as the provision of office accommodation where the rental is paid by a third party or the free use of telephone facilities) or services from volunteers. Such incoming resources should only be included in the SOFA where the benefit to the PCC is reasonably quantifiable and measurable. Donated services and facilities include those normally provided by an individual or entity as part of their trade or profession for a fee, but will exclude the value of contribution from volunteers as their contribution cannot be reasonably quantified in financial terms. The cost in the SOFA should be the estimated value to the PCC of the service or facility received. This will be the price the PCC estimates it would pay in the open market for a service or facility of equivalent utility to the PCC. An equivalent amount should be included in the SOFA as expenditure under the appropriate heading. As a result, both the value of this incoming resource and its contribution to the application of resources is recognised.

Most PCCs receive substantial amounts of voluntary help. Such help should not be accounted for in the SOFA, but should be gratefully acknowledged in the Annual Report, where it can also be quantified.

7.1.12 Donor-imposed restrictions

Where money is given to the PCC specifically to provide a fixed asset or where a fixed asset is donated (a gift in kind), the PCC will normally have entitlement to ownership and use of the gift at the point when it is receivable. At this point, the gift should be recognised in the SOFA and not deferred over the life of the asset. The possibility of having to repay the gift does not affect its recognition in the first place. Once acquired, the use of the asset will be either restricted or unrestricted. If the use is restricted the asset will be held in a restricted fund (as an endowment, to reflect the donor's intention of 'continuing' use). If its retention and use are unrestricted (i.e. the PCC is free to sell the asset and spend the proceeds for general purposes), the trustees may consider creating a designated fund to 'ring-fence' its carrying value from the PCC's 'free' reserves. The relevant fund (endowment or designated) should then be reduced over the useful economic life of the asset in line with its depreciation.

When a PCC receives a gift, bequest or grant it will account for it, in either an unrestricted or restricted fund, once it is entitled to it and there are no preconditions preventing its use. A condition that prevents entitlement and use must be one that is outside the PCC's control (such as obtaining offers of matched funding from a third party or that the funds may only be expended in a later accounting period). When such a condition applies, the receipt should not be included in the SOFA until the precondition has been met (i.e. until the money can lawfully be spent). The amount of such 'deferred income' will instead be shown in the balance sheet as a 'liability'. The financial statements notes should explain all movements in 'deferred income', to enable the reader to understand the implications.

7.1.13 Accounting for tax recoverable under the Gift Aid scheme

By the end of the year the PCC is likely to have received voluntary income on which tax can be reclaimed under the Gift Aid scheme. The tax claim for the year must be recognised in the financial statements in full within the fund to which the donation belongs, namely:

- any amounts that have been claimed and received from HMRC that relate to donations made to the PCC during the year;

- any amounts that have been claimed from HMRC but not yet received;

- any amounts that have yet to be claimed at the year end ('claimable').

Tax repayable to the PCC should be included in the SOFA in the same year as the income to which it relates, and even if disclosed separately as shown in the example, must be credited to the fund it belongs to – as stated above. Any such tax claim not received at the end of the year should be accounted for as a debtor until the PCC receives payment from HMRC.

7.1.14 Legacies

Legacies should be included in the SOFA in accordance with the general principles for the recognition of incoming resources.

Where the PCC is aware of an entitlement to a material legacy that for the above reason has not been included in the financial statements, this fact and an estimate of the amount receivable should be disclosed in the notes to the financial statements.

7.1.15 Grants receivable

Receipts by way of grant should be treated in a similar manner to other incoming resources. They should be dealt with in the SOFA in accordance with the terms of the grant. This means, for example, that grants intended for specific purposes should be accounted for as restricted funds – endowed or non-endowed as the case may be. Grants received as for ordinary activities of the PCC but which are then designated by the PCC to specific purposes should be included as receipts in unrestricted funds, and then shown in the SOFA as a transfer from unrestricted to designated funds.

Grants should not be recognised until the preconditions (if any) for their entitlement and use have been met. Once these preconditions are met, the grant should be recognised in the SOFA even if (as is normally the case) the resources are received in advance of related expenditure or if there is a condition that all or part of the donation may be repaid to the donor in specified circumstances. If repayment is possible then, depending on the probability, it should be noted as a contingent liability or recognised as an actual liability.

7.1.16 Trading activities

Some churches carry on trading activities such as letting church premises, selling books, producing magazines and running community cafés. Some of these activities may be outside the PCC's objects and care should be taken with major trading activities in case it is appropriate to form a separate trading company for liability and tax reasons. All proceeds of trading should be recognised as income of the year in which the 'sale' took place, and any associated costs should be included in expenditure at the same time. The accounting principles for the recognition of assets and of liabilities require all trading income to be recognised in the SOFA at the point where an asset of the PCC is created or liability settled (i.e. when the PCC makes the sale) and likewise all trading costs to be recognised in the SOFA at the point where the external liability arises or a reduction in PCC assets occurs (normally when goods are sold from stock or services purchased for fulfilment of a sale). Where goods are purchased in one year but not sold until a later year, they should be shown in the balance sheet as stocks, in current assets, and charged to expenditure when the sale takes place.

Trading that is part of the PCC's charitable objects to further the work of the church (such as income from hall letting for church purposes and the sale of religious books) should be separated from fundraising trading (such as selling postcards and souvenirs to tourists).

Some 'trading' involves merely the disposal of gifts in kind donated to the church (such as cakes for a cake stall or clothing for a rummage sale). In economic terms these are similar to trading and the proceeds should be accounted for as activities for generating funds.

Even if the cost of the trading activity is immaterial it is not acceptable simply to show the net trading result (profit or loss) in the SOFA.

If more than one trading activity is undertaken, then each significant activity should be separately disclosed, but this can be done in the notes.

All forms of trading should be recognised in this manner if significant.

7.1.17 Disposal of fixed assets used for the functioning of the PCC

Any net gain arising on disposal of fixed assets (the sale proceeds less the book value) previously used by the PCC for its functional purposes (such as the curate's house or the office photocopier) should be included in the SOFA as an incoming resource of the fund concerned. If a net loss arises for the year, it should be included as an additional depreciation charge to the fund concerned under the appropriate heading of charitable or other expenditure. If material, the gains and losses should be disclosed separately, with a supporting note by way of explanation.

7.1.18 Netting off

All incoming resources should, as far as practicable, be reported gross and not netted off against expenditure. This means, for example, that expenditure on putting on a fundraising event such as a fete should not be netted off against the funds raised. On occasions it may not be practicable to report the resources gross, i.e. if the event is not under the control of the PCC and it is merely a passive beneficiary of the net proceeds raised. In such a case the reason for netting off should be given in the notes and an estimate of the gross funds raised and the deducted expenditure given in the SOFA.

7.1.19 Cost of generating funds

Voluntary income raised by the PCC should be brought into account gross, and associated costs should be accounted for as fundraising expenditure.

7.1.20 Analysis

Chapter 2 provides an aid, and all the account descriptions that are used in keeping the accounts need not be separately included in the financial statements. The principle of materiality will decide which to show separately. An item is material and should be disclosed separately in the accounts if its misstatement or omission might reasonably be expected to influence the users of those accounts. Conversely, if too much detail is included, the understandability of the information given in the accounts can be impaired. It is therefore a judgement call by the trustees.

While smaller PCCs do not have to follow these activity headings, it is strongly recommended that they do so. This will make it easier for those who wish to compare PCC accounts and for the completion of annual Returns of Parish Finance (RPF) to the diocese or Archbishops' Council. The relevant RPF note number has been included alongside each account description.

The headings in the category column correspond to the SORP's requirements and should be disclosed on the face of the SOFA as needed. Only where the amount is material should an individual account heading be disclosed on either the face of the SOFA or in the notes. Account headings should not be disclosed even in the notes to the financial statements, unless they are considered material enough to do so.

7.2 The balance sheet

This section describes how assets and liabilities should be accounted for by PCCs. For accruals accounts the rules set out in the Charities SORP must be adopted as the PCC's general accounting policy.

7.2.1 Format

The Balance Sheet should be supported by notes. A full example, including notes summarising the movements in significant individual funds, is shown in Chapter 8.

The funds of a PCC should be grouped by kind, distinguishing between endowments, other restricted funds, designated and other unrestricted funds. The notes should distinguish any material individual funds among them and explain their nature and purpose.

In the notes to the balance sheet, the assets and liabilities representing the funds of the PCC should be clearly analysed fund by fund. The notes should indicate whether or not sufficient resources are held in an appropriate form to enable each fund to be applied in accordance with the restrictions (if any) imposed on it. For example, if a PCC has a fund that is to be spent in the near future, it should be made clear in the notes whether or not the assets held in the fund are short-term assets.

In addition, the assets and liabilities should be analysed in a way that enables the reader to gain a proper appreciation of their spread and character. PCCs should not feel restricted by the formats provided in this chapter and are expected to provide more detail or analysis of the items concerned where this will lead to a better understanding of the financial statements. For example, long-term debtors (i.e. due only after more than one year) should, where the total is material, be separately stated in the balance sheet – otherwise their total amounts by category should be disclosed in the notes to the financial statements.

7.2.2 Assets and their valuation

All assets of material value held for use on a continuing basis (i.e. two years or more) in the PCC's activities should be classified as fixed assets for PCC use and included in (or excluded from) the balance sheet. Most of these fixed assets are likely to be tangible assets, such as property or equipment, which are used in the course of the PCC's activities. Land and buildings held primarily for investment purposes should be classified as 'investment properties' and included with investments.

In order to account correctly for assets, PCCs need to understand what funds they hold in trust, what funds are held on their behalf for which they are responsible, and how they should value the assets of all these funds according to their use. In general terms, assets for which PCCs are responsible fall into the following groups for accounting purposes:

- intangible assets
- tangible fixed assets used for the work of the PCC:
  - land and buildings
  - motor vehicles
  - fixtures, fittings and equipment
- investment assets other than social (project-related) investments
- social (project-related) investment assets
- current assets.

7.2.3 Intangible assets

An example of these is copyright royalties. These are very rare in practice and so no detail is included here.

7.2.4 Tangible fixed assets used for the work of the PCC

Tangible fixed assets include land and buildings, both freehold and leasehold, other than those held primarily for investment purposes, and motor vehicles and fixtures, fittings and equipment.

The basic rule is found in the SORP's module 10: 'Tangible fixed assets must be measured initially on the balance sheet at their historical cost. All costs incurred to bring a tangible fixed asset into its intended working condition should be included in the measurement of cost. Charities may adopt an accounting policy of capitalising borrowing costs, including interest, that are directly attributable to the construction of tangible fixed assets, or may write off such borrowing costs as an expense in the SOFA as they are incurred.' FRS 102 says: 'A tangible fixed asset shall initially be measured at its cost, then written down to its recoverable amount if necessary.' The initial carrying amount of a tangible fixed asset received as a gift or donation by a charity shall be its fair value on the open market (or the trustees' best estimate thereof) as at the date of gift, which for a functional asset is its deemed historical cost under FRS 102. On first-time adoption of FRS 102, the PCC can choose to freeze the existing carrying value of any such asset as at the start of the prior financial year or else its fair value as at that date. Where there is no record of the purchase price or production cost of an asset, or any such record cannot be obtained without unreasonable expense or delay, the value ascribed must be the earliest available record of its value. Particulars must be given of any case where the purchase price or production cost of any asset is for the first time determined in this way.

Tangible fixed assets not carried at actual or deemed historical cost under FRS 102 must be carried at fair value, annually updated, and all assets of the same class treated in the same way. The accounts notes must disclose in respect of them:

● the effective date of the revaluation;

● whether an independent valuer was involved;

● the methods and significant assumptions applied in estimating the items' fair value;

● for each revalued class of property, plant and equipment, the carrying amount that would have been recognised had the assets been carried under the historical cost model.

Valuations may be obtained from a suitably qualified person, who could be a trustee or employee, for any class of fixed assets for which the PCC adopts a policy of accounting at 'fair value' instead of at historical cost as above. There are no other alternatives to these two bases (see 7.2.12 below).

A number of PCCs have assets, e.g. historic buildings that are used by the church, for example for worship, but valuing them when they have not been previously included in accounts for lack of reliable historical cost information might have been considered impractical prior to FRS 102. This would have been because reliable historical cost/value information is not available and alternative valuation approaches (such as using the current cost of construction) lack sufficient reliability (e.g. in ignoring land values) as a measure of 'fair value'. The FRS 102 'first-time transitioning' option solved that problem by offering a 'window of opportunity' to carry any individual functional fixed asset in the accounts at its 'deemed historical cost' equal to its estimated 'fair value' as at the start of the prior year. That fair value must distinguish the freehold land component (normally non-depreciating), from the buildings component, whose 'depreciable amount' (i.e. less their anticipated disposal value at current prices as if the buildings had now reached the end of their useful economic life) is to be expensed (unless it is immaterial) annually over the buildings' estimated remaining 'useful economic life' – which for a PCC will normally be based on their 'service potential'.

If, in such a case, that option has not been taken, and the asset is still not valued in the accounts, the notes should contain a statement to that effect, explaining the reasons why. The notes should also contain information that enables the reader to appreciate the age, scale and nature of the excluded assets and the use made of them and their present condition.

7.2.5 Depreciation of fixed assets held for the PCC's own use

Most tangible fixed assets depreciate; that is, wear out with the passing of time or become obsolete. Their value is thus expended over their useful economic life. This expenditure is recognised as depreciation in the SOFA and deducted from the asset's carrying value in the balance sheet.

Fixed assets held for functional (church) use that are included in the balance sheet and are considered to have a finite useful life should be depreciated at annual rates to spread their cost to the PCC evenly over their useful life in each case. An example of such assets is a computer used in the church office. In addition, if recently acquired movable church furnishings are included (because they have either been valued or recently acquired), they should also be depreciated. PCCs should set a threshold below which fixed assets are considered too small to include in the balance sheet ('capitalise'). Many PCCs set a threshold (of perhaps £500 or £1,000) below which fixed assets are included in expenditure rather than in the balance sheet.

This annual depreciation charge should be included in the appropriate cost category in the SOFA, and the accumulated depreciation will appear in the balance sheet as a deduction from the value of the relevant fixed assets.

To achieve the correct categorisation of depreciation if the activity-based presentation of expenditure is used in the SOFA, functional fixed assets should be divided between those used primarily in direct furtherance of the PCC's objects (for example, church halls and PCC-owned houses) and those used primarily used for raising funds (other than investment income, (where a house is made available for rental on the open market rather than for rental by PCC staff).

If a house is retained primarily to generate a market level of rent rather than for the church's own use, then it will be an investment property and will not be depreciated.

Where a fixed asset used for the functioning of the PCC and included at a carrying value in the balance sheet has suffered a permanent diminution by reference to the higher of its disposal value or its 'value in use' or 'service potential' (this is unlikely to be a frequent occurrence for PCCs), the loss should be recognised by means of an impairment charge in the SOFA, by way of additional depreciation.

In determining whether the balance sheet value of any individual asset has become 'impaired', changes in the value of other assets should not be taken into account.

The Church of England has complex rules about ownership of assets. PCCs may be trustees of income and expenditure relating to assets of which they are not the legal owner* and in relation to which they are not accountable under Part 8 of the Charities Act 2011. (*FRS 102 requires a 'substance over form' approach by defining 'assets' for inclusion in the accounts as 'resources controlled by the entity as a result of past events and from which future economic benefits are expected to flow to the entity'. This clearly goes beyond legal ownership unless exclusion is statutory.) Most PCCs will be in the following position with regard to their tangible fixed assets:

7.2.6 Land and Buildings

Benefice property (e.g. parsonage houses) will appear as assets of the Board of Finance and therefore will not be in the accounts of the PCC.

Where a parish has other buildings, the legal title to these are vested in a diocesan body as custodian trustee (PCC are the managing trustees). As fixed assets of the PCC that are held for continuing use in its work, these should all be included in the balance sheet and shown under the appropriate fund heading to indicate which fund they belong to.

Consecrated land/buildings and equipment are not included in the financial statements by virtue of Charities Act 2011. In law 'consecration' is not considered to be the same as 'dedication' as the latter is no more than an expression of pious intention that the building or land is given back to God. By act of consecration, property is effectively dedicated to God and set aside solely for sacred purposes. Costs associated with the maintenance or improvement of such assets will be written off in the year they are incurred.

Land and buildings can be left at an existing valuation or revalued to 'fair value' as at 1 January, 2015 which will then be the deemed historical cost. Apart from that, if a revaluation policy is subsequently adopted it must be for all assets within that asset-class, with the carrying values updated on a regular basis, and the trustees may use any reasonable approach to valuation at least every five years, with reviews in between to consider if there have been any material changes.

Great care should therefore be taken not to miss this opportunity if the PCC has hitherto been using the insured value for balance sheet valuation purposes, unless the insurance is for only the fair value of the asset taking into account its existing condition (i.e. 'total loss' replacement cost less a deduction for wear and tear to date) and the current land value (for existing use) is added in. The value in a 'replacement as new' policy would need to be modified to bring it to a fair value.

Building and leasehold properties will need to be depreciated over their estimated useful lives in accordance with a disclosed policy. A policy of non-depreciation can only be adopted if both the annual depreciation charge and the accumulated depreciation are immaterial to the financial statements, due to the asset having a very long remaining useful life (i.e. 50 years or more), and/ or the currently estimated residual value is high. The assessment of residual value has changed significantly under SORP (FRS 102). As the glossary to FRS 102 says, the 'residual value' is: 'The estimated amount that an entity would currently obtain from disposal of an asset, after deducting the estimated costs of disposal, if the asset were already of the age and in the condition expected at the end of its useful life.' This means pretending that the building in question is not fit for purpose as far as the PCC is concerned but has been maintained in good order up to the year end, and then estimating the price an informed purchaser would pay for that building as it stands, plus its land. After stripping out that land value (as non-depreciable), the building's residual value for depreciation purposes will normally be considerably higher than when it had to be assessed by reference to prices ruling at the time of its acquisition or last revaluation. This could in turn significantly reduce annual depreciation charges, going forward.

If no depreciation is charged, on the basis of immateriality, then an impairment review must be undertaken annually. This need not be onerous as it seeks to establish some indication that the amount an asset is carried at on the balance sheet is less than both of the sale value, or the value of the use the asset provides to the parish.

Freehold land must not be depreciated.

7.2.7 Motor vehicles and fixtures, fittings and equipment

The various items of movable church furnishings are vested in the churchwardens for the use and benefit of the parishioners and cannot be disposed of without a faculty. These assets are regarded as 'inalienable' property held on special trust on behalf of the PCC, and (unless forming part of the consecrated property excluded from accounts by the Charities Act) should be capitalised and disclosed in the fixtures, fittings and equipment asset category under the appropriate fund.

In addition to fixtures, fittings and equipment described above, the parish will have 'functional equipment' that is used on a continuing basis for the work of the PCC. Examples include: office equipment (computers etc.), ground and building maintenance equipment and vehicles. These are fixed assets and (apart from any immaterial items that have been treated as an expense) should be included in the balance sheet – this will normally be at cost less depreciation.

The notes to the financial statements should also summarise all changes in the amounts of each category of fixed assets as shown in the balance sheet and reconcile the opening and closing balances on each one. This means separate reconciliations of the cost to date (or the valuation, where the 'current value' option under the accounting standards has been chosen since 2000) and of the depreciation or amortisation provided. Similarly, the notes should show the movements in investment fixed assets.

7.2.8 Investment fixed assets

Investment fixed assets include properties held wholly or primarily for investment purposes, as well as investment securities and long-term cash deposits. Investment fixed assets must be valued at their open market value (where practicable) unless made in furtherance of a charitable purpose, in which case as 'social investments' they should be carried at historical cost less any amounts now deemed irrecoverable. This would include 'soft loans' made for church purposes.

7.2.9 Current assets

Current assets include stocks (gifted stock cost equals fair value) (of paper, cards etc.), debtors, investment assets currently held for disposal without reinvestment and cash at bank and in hand. They should be recognised at the lower of their cost and their net realisable value – other than investment assets (see paragraph 7.2.8 above). Current assets should be subdivided by category, where applicable, to show:

● stock (for example heating oil, bookstall publications);

● debtors, which should be further analysed in the notes between:

  – debtors for goods and services (for example rents receivable on premises letting);

  – amounts owed by an institution or body corporate that is a related party to the PCC;

  – other debtors (for example amounts owed by HMRC);

  – prepayments and accrued income;

● investment assets (only applicable where the PCC intends to spend the proceeds of sale on activities instead of reinvesting them);

● cash at bank and in hand (including deposits with the CCLA Church of England Funds or a Diocesan Board of Finance).

The notes applicable to showing the movement in investment assets held as fixed assets also apply to investment assets held as current assets – which the SORP also requires to be shown at their current market value, even if this exceeds their historical cost.

7.2.10 Current liabilities and long-term liabilities

Current liabilities include loans and overdrafts, trade creditors, amounts owed to subsidiary undertakings, other creditors and accrued expenses and deferred income. They should be recognised on the balance sheet at their settlement value. Amounts due after more than one year should be separately disclosed at their present value unless the difference is immaterial.

Liabilities should be analysed between those payable within a year (short-term) and others (long-term), with the total (if material) of any provisions for liabilities shown separately.

The totals for both short-term and long-terms liabilities should be sub-analysed in the notes between:

● loans and overdrafts;

● creditors for goods and services;

● amounts owed to any institution or body corporate that is a related party to the PCC;

● accrued expenses and deferred income (e.g. an estimate of fuel unbilled up to the year end);

● If a PCC has not fully paid its parish share but has indicated to the DBF that it intends to make further payment towards the outstanding amount, that payment should be included as a creditor in the balance sheet. If for whatever reason a PCC's full parish share is not to be met, this fact should be mentioned in the Annual Report to enable a full understanding of the PCC's financial affairs.

7.2.11 **Heritage assets**

Heritage assets are assets of historical or artistic importance that are held primarily to advance preservation, conservation and educational objectives of charities and in order through public access to contribute in themselves to the nation's culture and education either at national or local level. Such assets are central to the achievement of the purposes of such charities and include the land, buildings, structures, collections, exhibits or artefacts that are preserved or conserved and are central to the educational objectives of such charities. The primary objective of any PCC is not the preservation of the buildings they occupy or the furnishings and other artefacts for which they are responsible, and none of a PCC's assets will therefore be heritage assets, even though some may be of considerable historical or artistic importance.

7.2.12 **Accounting bases**

The methods and principles on which assets are to be included in the balance sheet are illustrated in the model set of accounting policies.

CATEGORY	CLASS	RECOGNITION	VALUATION
Intangible assets		Include if purchased	Historical cost
Tangible fixed assets	Consecrated property	Not included in accounts May note existence in TAR	No valuation required
	Freehold land and buildings (e.g. PCC-owned house, church hall)	Include	Cost (or deemed cost) or fair value, less depreciation (no depreciation on land)
	Leasehold land and buildings Motor vehicles Fixtures, fittings and equipment – including movable church furnishings (unless forming part of 'consecrated property')	Include	Cost (or deemed cost) or fair value, less depreciation
Investment fixed assets	Investment properties Financial investments securities Long-term cash deposits	Include	Fair value
Social investments	Securities; 'soft' loans	Include	Historical cost less irrecoverable amounts
Current assets	Investments shortly to be disposed of for spending	Include	Fair value
Current assets	Stock Debtors Cash at bank/in hand	Include	Lower of cost (or gift value) and net realisable value
Liabilities and long-term creditors	Loans and overdrafts Other creditors Accruals and deferred income	Include	The value at which the liability will be settled (reduced to present value)

7.3 Cash flow statement

Introduction

If the PCCs income for the year exceeds £500,000, the PCC is deemed to be a 'larger charity'. There are extra disclosure requirements for the Annual Report and the accounts and a cash flow statement is mandatory under FRS 102.

The statement of cash flows provides information about how the PCC has used cash generated by its activities or financed its cash needs. It thus provides information that is helpful in assessing the liquidity but not necessarily the solvency of the funds of the PCC, for which the balance sheet and its supporting accounts notes are needed. Liquidity means the ability to meet immediate and short-term obligations and solvency means also all longer-term obligations (i.e. to remain solvent, the anticipated realisable value of all assets must exceed all liabilities).

The statement identifies the PCC's cash flows in three basic categories and the net increase or decrease in cash or cash equivalents for those categories in the reporting period. Cash equivalents are defined as short-term, highly liquid investments that are readily convertible into known amounts of cash and that are subject to an insignificant risk of change in value. Highly liquid investments normally have a maturity of three months or less from the date of acquisition.

Bank overdrafts repayable on demand form an integral part of day-to-day cash management and are thus a component of cash and cash equivalents. Other forms of cash advance that are less flexible than overdraft, such as term loans, always count as part of borrowings and are categorised as financing activities.

Structure of the statement of cash flows

The format of the statement of cash flows must follow the requirements of section 7 of FRS 102. The statement must analyse cash flows using three standard headings: operating activities; investing activities; financing activities. The statement includes the movement in cash balances of unrestricted funds and also of restricted funds, meaning trust funds, including all endowment capital as well as all donor-restricted (i.e. special-purpose) income funds. An example statement of cash flows is provided at the end of this chapter. A PCC must prepare a statement of cash flows on a consolidated basis where applicable.

What cash flows are included as operating activities?

Operating activities are the day-to-day mission-related and income-producing activities of the PCC that are recognised as income and expenditure in the SOFA. Thus they do not include any internal or external inflow or outflow of endowment cash, which instead must be included in the investing and financing sections (see below). The net cash flow of operating activities indicates the extent to which operating activities have generated or consumed cash. Examples of cash flows of operating activities would therefore include:

- Parish contributions, Archbishops' Council grants and other donations/grants;

- Statutory fees, chaplaincy income and other income earned from charitable activities;

- Receipt of rents from parsonage houses;

- Cash payments of grants made;

- Cash payments to suppliers of goods and services;

- Cash payments to and on behalf of staff (for example, diocesan staff salaries, clergy stipends and pension contributions);

What cash flows are included as investing activities?

Investing activities include payments for the acquisition of investments and receipts from their disposal (either for reinvestment or as divestment) as well as the cash generated as income from holding investment assets, but the latter excludes those highly liquid investments which are classed as cash equivalents. This section also includes payments for the acquisition of, or receipts from the disposal of, tangible fixed assets including property, plant or equipment.

It is worth noting here that the special treatment needed for endowment cash flows, as distinct from those of 'operating activities', was explained in paragraph 354 of SORP 2005, which (with terminology updated) said:

> *'Movements in endowments should not be included in cash flows from 'operating activities' but should be treated as increases or decreases in the financing section. This is achieved as follows: ...*
>
> *(b) the receipts and payments from the acquisition and disposal of investments should be shown gross in the 'investing' section of the cash flow statement. A single row should then be included in this section showing the net movement in cash flows attributable to endowment investments. A corresponding row should be included in the 'financing' section for the same amount. The row in the 'financing' section should reflect the cash into/(cash out of) the endowment fund whereas it will be the opposite direction in the 'investing' section; ...'.*

Examples of cash flows arising from a DBF's investing activities thus include;

- Cash receipts from interest and dividends received;

- Cash receipts from rent on investment properties including revenues from Glebe land;

- Cash receipts from the repayment of loans by a non-charitable trading subsidiary;

- Cash receipts from the sale of plant, property and equipment and other long-term assets;

- Cash receipts from the sale of investment properties and other long-term investments (including the sale of endowment investments);

- As an internal cash inflow from the financing section (see below) any endowment capital either borrowed or converted into income, less any internal cash outflow to that section in respect of all investment income from a permanent endowment to which a duly authorised 'total return' investing policy applies;

- Cash payments to acquire investments (including conversion of endowment to another form of investment – e.g. investment property instead of functional property, etc.); and

- Cash payments to acquire tangible fixed assets, including property and equipment and other long-term assets (including conversion of endowment to another form of fixed asset – e.g. functional property instead of investment property).

What cash flows are included as financing activities?

'Financing' activities comprise borrowings and their repayment, but also any gifts to the DBF of permanent endowments or expendable endowments. Endowment funds are considered to be 'capital' in charity law, as they must be retained and (unless comprising functional fixed assets) invested for a financial return.

Examples of cash flows arising from financing activities thus include:

- Cash receipts representing donations of endowment capital;

- As *internal* cash inflows from the investing section (see above), the accumulation as capital of (i) cash from operational activities under a power to create expendable endowment and/or (ii) cash received as investment income from a permanent endowment under a duly authorised total return investing policy, less the duly authorised conversion of any endowment capital into income for operating activities or any internal borrowing from permanent capital (less related recoupments to capital);

● Cash receipts from new external borrowings by way of loan or mortgage and other long- or short-term borrowings;

● Cash receipts from the use of a bank overdraft facility (if not treated as a component of cash equivalents);

● Cash repayments of external borrowing including mortgages, loans and other borrowing;

● Cash payments by a lessee which reduce the outstanding liability relating to a finance lease.

The methods of compiling the statement of cash flows

FRS 102 permits charities to use either the direct or indirect method when presenting the cash flow from operating activities. The indirect method is most commonly used and is the method illustrated in the example at the end of this chapter.

A PCC can choose to present the statement of cash flows using either:

● The indirect method, which involves deriving from the SOFA the figure of net cash flows of operating activities. The net movement in funds shown in the SOFA is adjusted for:

● Non-cash movements in the SOFA;

● Any accounting deferrals or accruals related to cash receipts or payments;

● Items of income or expenditure related to 'investing or financing cash flows'; or:

● The direct method, whereby the gross cash receipts and gross cash payments are disclosed for each of the main categories shown in the SOFA. This method has the merit of making the DBF's operational receipts and payments clear to the general reader unversed in the niceties of accruals-based financial reporting, and the demerit that cash flows do not necessarily reflect the true financial position and performance.

Example statement of cash flows

The example statement of cash flows shown at the end of this chapter uses the indirect method. When using this method, a reconciliation must be provided to show how the net income/(expenditure) presented in the SOFA has been adjusted to arrive the cash flows from operating activities. An example of this reconciliation is shown, together with a reconciliation of cash and cash equivalents.

The example must be adapted as necessary for any additional items that apply. An example would be cash flows arising from the payment of taxes. Similarly, headings that do not apply must be omitted.

When significant cash or cash equivalents are held which are not available for use to further charitable activities, for example those held in endowment funds, the charity must disclose;

● The amount unavailable; and

● Explain why it is unavailable for use

Examples of financing transactions include the conversion of expendable endowment into income funds in advance of the relevant investments being sold, or the removal of the legal restriction on the expenditure of permanent endowment enabling it to be spent in the future.

If the components of cash and cash equivalents presented in the statement of cash flows are different to the equivalent items in the charity's balance sheet, a reconciliation must be provided.

ST LEDGER'S, AMBRIDGE PAROCHIAL CHURCH COUNCIL

STATEMENT OF CASH FLOWS

For the year ending 31 December 20XX

	20XX	20XX
	£000	£000
Cash flows from operating activities:		
Net cash provided by (used in) operating activities	(xxx)	(xxx)
Cash flows from investing activities:		
Dividends, interest and rents from investments	xxx	xxx
Proceeds from the sale of property, plant and equipment	xxx	xxx
Purchase of property, plant and equipment	(xxx)	(xxx)
Proceeds from sales of investments	–	xxx
Purchase of investments	(xxx)	(xxx)
Net cash in/(out)flow internally in respect of endowment capital	(xxx)	(xxx)
Net cash provided by (used in) investing activities	(xxx)	xx
Cash flows from financing activities:		
Repayments of borrowing	(xx)	(xx)
Cash inflows from new borrowing	xxx	xxx
Receipt of endowment	xx	–
Net cash in/(out)flow internally in respect of endowment capital	xxx	xxx
Net cash provided by (used in) financing activities	xxx	xxx
Change in cash and cash equivalents in the reporting period	(xxx)	(xx)
Cash and cash equivalents at 1 January 20xx	x,xxx	xxx
Cash and cash equivalents at 31 December 20xx	xxx	x,xxx
Reconciliation of net movements in funds to net cash flow from operating activities		
Net movement in funds for the year ended 31 December 20xx	xxx	xx
Adjustments for:		
Depreciation charges	xx	xx
Dividends, interest and rents from investments	(xxx)	(xxx)
Repayments of loans advanced	xxx	xxx
Advancement of loans	(xxx)	(xxx)
Loss/(profit) on sale of fixed assets	(xx)	(xx)
(Increase)/decrease in stocks	(x)	x
(Increase)/decrease in debtors	(xxx)	xxx
Increase in creditors	xxx	xx
Net cash provided by (used in) operating activities	(xxx)	(xxx)
Analysis of cash and cash equivalents		
Cash in hand	xxx	x,xxx
Notice deposits (less than 3 months)	xx	–
Overdraft facility payable on demand	xx x	xxx x

chapter 8

Financial Statements (Accruals Accounting) Example

ANNUAL REPORT AND FINANCIAL STATEMENTS

For the year ended 31 December 2016

The Parochial Church Council of St Ledger's Church, Ambridge

Registered Charity number 1234567

The Parochial Church Council of St Ledger's Church, Barchester

EXAMPLE TRUSTEES' ANNUAL REPORT (ACCRUALS ACCOUNTING)

2016 Report and Accounts for the Parochial Church Council of St Ledger's Church, Ambridge

Aim and purposes

St Ledger's Parochial Church Council (PCC) has the responsibility of cooperating with the incumbent, the Reverend James Colossae, in promoting in the ecclesiastical parish, the whole mission of the church, pastoral, evangelistic, social and ecumenical. The PCC is also specifically responsible for the maintenance of the Church Centre complex of St Ledger's, The Green, Ambridge.

Objectives and activities

The PCC is committed to enabling as many people as possible to worship at our church and to become part of our parish community at St Ledger. The PCC maintains an overview of worship throughout the parish and makes suggestions on how our services can involve the many groups that live within our parish. Our services and worship put faith into practice through prayer and Scripture, music and sacrament.

When planning our activities for the year, we have considered the Charity Commission's guidance on public benefit and, in particular, the supplementary guidance on charities for the advancement of religion. In particular, we try to enable ordinary people to live out their faith as part of our parish community through:

- Worship and prayer; learning about the gospel; developing their knowledge and trust in Jesus

- Provision of pastoral care for people living in the parish

- Missionary and outreach work.

To facilitate this work, it is important that we maintain the fabric of the church of St Ledger and the Church Centre complex.

Achievements and performance

Worship and prayer

The PCC is keen to offer a range of services during the week and over the course of the year that our community find both beneficial and spiritually fulfilling. For example, evening prayers provide a quiet, intimate and reflective environment for worship, while opportunities are provided for people to engage in more outgoing worship such as that provided by the youth group within our parish.

This year we have been successful in welcoming more families into our church and have agreed a new style of family worship on the morning of the third Sunday each month. This has meant that special arrangements have had to be made for baptisms and for welcoming the families at corporate worship on the first Sunday of each month. It is pleasing to be able to report that the new arrangements have been well received since they came into operation during September. They will be reviewed by the PCC after 12 months. In addition, a great deal of time and thought was spent during the year on making best use of the new services. Many have said how much easier it is to follow the services now that they are printed out in booklets.

All are welcome to attend our regular services. At present there are 173 parishioners on the church electoral roll, 91 of whom are not resident within the parish. Eighteen names were added during the year and nine were removed either through death or because they moved away from the parish. The average weekly attendance, counted during October, was 107, but this number increased at festivals, and two Christmas carol services had to be held to seat all those who wished to attend.

As well as our regular services, we enable our community to celebrate and thank God at the milestones of the journey through life. Through baptism we thank God for the gift of life; in marriage public vows are exchanged with God's blessing; through funeral services friends and family express their grief and give thanks for the life which is now complete in this world, and commend the person into God's keeping. We have celebrated 25 baptisms and 15 weddings and held 26 funerals in our church this year.

Deanery Synod

Three members of the PCC sit on the Deanery Synod. This provides the PCC with an important link between the parish and the wider structures of the Church. This year the PCC has also focused its attention on the questions posed to parishes in the deanery about the most effective deployment of stipendiary and non-stipendiary clergy.

The Church Centre complex

We want our church to be open to our community for private prayer. Unfortunately, since the theft of valuable church artefacts from St Augustus' Church, in the neighbouring parish, we have felt unable to leave the church open at all times for private worship. We are, however, pleased that a rota of parishioners has enabled us to open the church at weekends and for all public holidays in the past year.

The state of the nave roof had been identified as a major concern for some time and despite routine maintenance being carried out, a detailed report on its condition prepared by the architect in April 2015 confirmed the need for major structural renewal and re-ordering. The work started in January 2016 and the total cost of the project was £189,000. Grants totalling £162,000 were received and a further £8,000 was raised from fundraising. The PCC had decided not to start an appeal and would instead fund the shortfall of £19,000 from general funds (£10,000 had been designated in the previous year).

The kitchen in the church hall was refurbished during August and the new environment meets the stringent health and safety requirements and allows us to continue the old people's luncheon club on Saturdays. Eighteen people regularly attend at our luncheon club, twelve of whom are parishioners. We were particularly pleased to be able to extend the services of our club to the members of the Ambridge Green Methodist Chapel luncheon club when the death of Alice Luther, the main organiser of that club, forced its closure.

During the week the hall is used by our mothers and toddlers group on Wednesdays. Fifteen children and their carers have been regular attenders at the mother and toddler group. During the summer the group organised two outings including older siblings during the school holidays. In July, 20 children and their parents went for the day to Longleat and later in the holidays we had the hottest day of the year for our family outing to New Milton.

The crèche runs in the hall on Tuesday and Thursday mornings. There are 12 regular attenders at the crèche, which is organised by Sally Pincent, the council's peripatetic childcare co-ordinator who runs crèches at our church as well as at St Augustus' on Mondays and Wednesdays. She has a rota of volunteers from the parish who help her, all of whom have been CRB checked. The crèche had an OFSTED inspection during the year and passed with flying colours.

Pastoral care

Some members of our parish are unable to attend church due to sickness or age. Reverend James Colossae has visited all church members who have requested it, to celebrate communion with them either at their homes or in hospital. Miss Finching has continued to organise a rota of volunteers to visit all who are sick or unable to get out for any other reason, to keep them in touch with church life.

Mission and evangelism

Helping those in need is a demonstration of our faith. The Mission and Evangelism Committee is to be congratulated on its fundraising efforts. Missionary and charitable giving totalled £56,200. Three members of our congregation are working with the Moses Cain and Grace Cross charity, which works with deprived children in the Far East. Thanks to the generosity of the congregation and the tireless work of John Leighton in securing grants, we were able to send £38,650 to support their work. £11,200 has been raised during the year to continue the support to CMS and £3,500 for the Ambridge Pensioners' Club. Additionally, this year £2,850 was raised for the Southern Africa Famine appeal.

Our parish magazine is distributed quarterly to all parishioners on the church electoral roll and is available at the church hall. The magazine keeps our parishioners informed of the important matters affecting our church and articles that help develop our knowledge and trust in Jesus.

Ecumenical relationships

The church is a member of Churches Together in Ambridge and of the Wessex Interfaith Forum. We have held joint services on the fourth Sunday of every month with the Ambridge Green Methodist Church, and for the first time this year have joined with them both for our Lent courses and to run an Alpha course in the autumn. The Alpha course has led a number of people to attend other church activities and services. We have also worked with Ambridge Green Methodist Church and Millfield Baptist Church to deliver a flyer to every home in the town advertising the Christmas services of all three churches.

Financial review

Total receipts on unrestricted funds were £193,650, of which £107,900 was unrestricted planned voluntary donations, and a further £24,050 was from Gift Aid. Restricted grants and donations of £216,750 were also received, the majority of which was for the major structural renewal project, and details are shown in the financial statements. The freehold house at 36 Church Street continues to be let temporarily, which provided a gross income of £4,200.

The planned giving through envelopes and banker's orders increased by 9% and it was good to see that the use of Gift Aid envelopes increased. Total income, excluding legacies and exceptional income for the major structural renewal project went up by a healthy 13% compared with last year. This was mainly due to our stewardship campaign, whose theme was to give in grace, our time, talents and giving to reflect our deepening faith. We were grateful for a pecuniary legacy of £11,000 from the estate of Mrs Mary Rudge. £2,000 was set aside towards the cost of the much needed cleaning of the organ. The work was completed in time for Christmas.

£154,300 was spent from unrestricted funds to provide the Christian ministry from St Ledger's Church, including the contribution to the diocesan parish share that increased by 5% in the year and largely provides the stipends and housing for the clergy.

The sum that the churches in the deanery have to find is shared between the churches according to a formula that is based mainly on a head count of the congregations. We have to find more of the sum at St Ledger's as the size of our congregation increased more compared with other churches.

Net movement in funds on unrestricted funds was £24,305 including £5,000 surplus on the sale of investments. There was a small overspend on the restricted funds of £6,225. During the year, the total fund balances increased from £75,185 to £93,510, of which £83,240 is unrestricted.

Reserves policy

It is PCC policy to try to maintain a balance on free reserves (net current assets) which equates to at least three months unrestricted payments. This is equivalent to £39,000. It is held to smooth out fluctuations in cash flow and to meet emergencies. The balance of the free reserves at the year end was £45,885 which is marginally higher than this target.

The balance of £7,775 in the restricted fund is retained towards meeting the upkeep of the Church Hall.

It is our policy to invest the short term investment fund balances with the CCLA Church of England Deposit Fund, and the remainder in the CCLA Church of England Investment Fund.

Volunteers

We would like to thank all the volunteers who work so hard to make our church the lively and vibrant community it is. In particular, we want to mention our churchwardens Mrs Cartwright and Mr Jones, who have worked so tirelessly on our behalf, and Mrs Nunn, who has helped us all to understand the church's accounts and its finances.

Structure, governance and management

The Parochial Church Council is a corporate body established by the Church of England. The PCC operates under the Parochial Church Council Powers Measure. The PCC is a Registered Charity.

The method of appointment of PCC members is set out in the Church Representation Rules. At St Ledger's the membership of the PCC consists of the incumbent (our vicar), churchwardens, the reader and members elected by those members of the congregation who are on the electoral roll of the church. All those who attend our services/members of the congregation are encouraged to register on the electoral roll and stand for election to the PCC.

The PCC members are responsible for making decisions on all matters of general concern and importance to the parish, including deciding on how the funds of the PCC are to be spent. New members receive initial training into the workings of the PCC.

The full PCC met six times during the year with an average level of attendance of 80%. Given its wide responsibilities the PCC has a number of committees each dealing with a particular aspect of parish life. These committees, which include worship, mission and outreach and fabric and finance, are all responsible to the PCC and report back to it regularly, minutes of their decisions being received by the full PCC and discussed as necessary.

Related Parties

Donations from related parties (PCC members) included £7,250 restored to the major structural renwal project.

Administrative information

St. Ledger's Church is situated in The Green, Ambridge. It is part of the Diocese of Wessex within the Church of England. The correspondence address is The Vicarage, Church Street, Ambridge. Registered charity number 123456.

PCC members who have served at any time from 1 January 2012 until the date this report was approved are:

Ex officio members:

Incumbent:	The Reverend James Colossae (chairman)
Reader:	Mr Geoffrey Amis
Wardens:	Mrs Jean Cartwright
	Mr David Jones (vice chairman)

Elected members:

Mr Alex Tipshaw, representative on Deanery Synod

Mr Peter Ackworth (Secretary), representative on Deanery Synod

Mr Jack Pierce, representative on Deanery Synod

Miss Fiona Fielding (from 5 April 2006) Mrs Chloe Nunn (treasurer)

Mr Gary Gledhill

Miss Henrietta Gordon, Mrs Tina Foster

Miss Hermione Ward (until 5 April 2006) Mr Martin Ward

Miss Emily Airedale

Mr Julian Footbridge (until 5 April 2006) Miss Lizzie Wrexham

Mr Ronald Nicholas (from 5 April 2006)

Approved by the PCC on 1 March 2007 and signed on their behalf by the Reverend James Colossae (PCC Chairman)

Independent Examiner's Report to the Trustees of St Ledger's Parochial Church Council

I report on the accounts of the church for the year ended 31 December 2016 which are set out on pages xx to xx.

Respective Responsibilities of Trustees and Examiner

The church's trustees are responsible for the preparation of the accounts. The church's trustees consider that an audit is not required for this year under section 144(2) of the Charities Act 2011 (the 2011 Act)) and that an independent examination is needed.

It is my responsibility to:

● Examine the accounts under section 145 of the 2011 Act);

● To follow the procedures laid down in the General Directions given by the Charity Commissioners (under section 145(5)(b) of the 2011 Act); and

● To state whether particular matters have come to my attention.

Basis of Independent Examiner's report

My examination was carried out in accordance with the general Directions given by the Charity Commission. An examination includes a review of the accounting records kept by the charity and a comparison of the accounts presented with those records. It also includes consideration of any unusual items or disclosures in the accounts, and seeking explanations from you as trustees concerning any such matters. The procedures undertaken do not provide all the evidence that would be required in an audit and consequently no opinion is given as to whether the accounts present a 'true and fair view' and the report is limited to those matters set out in the statement below.

Independent examiner's statement

Since the gross income for the year exceeds the amount provided in section 145(3) of the Act, I confirm that I am qualified to act as Independent Examiner under the provisions of that section of the Act and that my qualification is as shown below.

In connection with my examination, no matter has come to my attention:

1. which gives me reasonable cause to believe that in any material respect the requirements

   ● to keep accounting records in accordance with section 130 of the 2011 Act; and

   ● to prepare accounts which accord with the accounting records and comply with the accounting requirements of the 2011 Act have not been met; or

2. to which, in my opinion, attention should be drawn in order to enable a proper understanding of the accounts to be reached.

(Name) (Date)

(Relevant professional qualification or body)

(Address)

Example Trustees' Annual Accounts (Accruals accounting)

SOFA

PAROCHIAL CHURCH COUNCIL OF ST LEDGER'S, AMBRIDGE

STATEMENT OF FINANCIAL ACTIVITIES

For the year ending 31 December 2016

	Note	Unrestricted funds £	Restricted funds £	Endowment funds £	TOTAL 2016 £	TOTAL 2015 £
INCOME AND ENDOWMENTS						
Voluntary income	2(a)	160,400	216,750	–	377,150	148,750
Activities for generating funds	2(b)	14,200	–	–	14,200	7,950
Income from investments	2(c)	3,250	2,500	–	5,750	5,100
Church activities	2(d)	15,800	–	–	15,800	13,150
TOTAL INCOME		193,650	219,250	–	412,900	174,950
EXPENDITURE						
Church activities	3(a)	154,300	244,275	–	398,575	161,275
Raising funds	3(b)	550	1,250	-	1,800	500
TOTAL EXPENDITURE		155,800	245,525	–	401,325	162,450
NET INCOME/(EXPENDITURE) BEFORE INVESTMENT GAINS		37,850	(26,275)	–	11,575	12,500
NET GAINS ON INVESTMENTS	7(b) & 8(a)	5,455	1,050	245	6,750	500
NET INCOME/(EXPENDITURE)		43,305	(25,225)	245	6,750	500
TRANSFER BETWEEN FUNDS	6	(19,000)	19,000	–	–	–
NET MOVEMENT IN FUNDS		24,305	(6,225)	245	18,325	13,000
Total funds brought forward	11	58,935	14,000	2,250	75,185	62,185
Total funds carried forward	12	**83,240**	7,775	2,495	93,510	75,185

PAROCHIAL CHURCH COUNCIL OF ST LEDGER'S, AMBRIDGE

BALANCE SHEET AT 31 DECEMBER 2016

	Notes	2016 £	2015 £
FIXED ASSETS			
Tangible	7(a)	34,000	37,000
Investments	7(b)	13,625	14,500
		47,625	51,500
CURRENT ASSETS			
Stock		150	150
Investments	8(a)	24,060	15,000
Debtors and prepayments	8(b)	9,675	4,000
Short-term deposits		11,000	8,000
Cash at bank and in hand		4,200	1,985
		49,085	29,135
LIABILITIES			
Creditors – amounts falling due within one year	9	2,700	4,450
NET CURRENT ASSETS/(LIABILITIES)		46,385	24,685
TOTAL ASSETS LESS CURRENT LIABILITIES		94,010	76,185
Creditors – amounts falling due after one year	9	500	1,000
TOTAL NET ASSETS		93,510	75,185
PARISH FUNDS			
Unrestricted	10	83,240	58,935
Restricted	10	7,775	14,000
Endowment	10	2,495	2,250
		93,510	75,185

Approved by the Parochial Church Council on 1 March 2017 and signed on its behalf by:
The Revd James Colossae (PCC chairman)

The notes on pages xx to xx form part of these accounts

PAROCHIAL CHURCH COUNCIL OF ST LEDGER'S, AMBRIDGE

CASH FLOW STATEMENT AT 31 DECEMBER 2016

	2016		2015	
	£	£	£	£
Net cash from operating activities		(3,300)		1,951
Cash flows from investing activities				
Dividends, interest and rent from investments	9,950		8,800	
Interest paid	0		0	
Proceeds from the sale of:				
Tangible fixed assets	0		0	
Tangible fixed investments	9,170		0	
Purchase of:				
Tangible fixed assets for the use of the PCC	0		0	
Fixed asset investments	(10,605)		(6,000)	
Net cash provided by/(used in) investing activities		8,515		2,80
Change in cash and cash equivalents in the				
reporting period		5,215		4,751
Cash and cash equivalents at 1 January		9,985		5,23
Cash and cash equivalents at 31 December		15,200		9,985
Reconciliation of net income/(expenditure)				
before investment gains				
Net income before investment gains 31 December		11,575		12,500
Adjustments for:				
Depreciation charges		3,000		3,000
Dividends, interest and rent from investments		(9,950)		(8,800)
Decrease/(increase) in debtors		(5,675)		(4,200)
(Decrease)/Increase in creditors		(2,250)		(549)
Net cash provided by/(used in) operating activities		(3,300)		1,951
Analysis of cash and cash equivalents				
Cash in hand		4,200		1,985
Notice deposits (less than 3 months)		11,000		8,000
		15,200		9,985

Although this is not required in this example, it is hown for illustrative purposes for those PCCs whose annual income is over £500,000.

PAROCHIAL CHURCH COUNCIL OF ST LEDGER'S, AMBRIDGE

NOTES TO THE FINANCIAL STATEMENTS For the year ended 31 December 2016 (continued)

1 ACCOUNTING POLICIES

The PCC is a public benefit entity within the meaning of FRS102. The financial statements have been prepared under the Charities Act 2011 and in accordance with the Church Accounting Regulations 2006 governing the individual accounts of PCCs, and with the Regulations' "true and fair view" provisions, it is also the first year that they have been prepared under FRS102 (2016) as the applicable accounting standards and the 2016 version of the Statement of Recommended Practice, Accounting and Reporting by Charities (SORP(FRS102)).

ASSETS

Consecrated and benefice property
In so far as consecrated and benefice property of any kind is excluded from the statutory definition of 'charity' by Section 10(2)(a) and (c) of the Charities Act 2011 such assets are not capitalised in the financial statements.

Moveable church furnishings
These are capitalised at cost and depreciated over their useful economic life other than where insufficient cost information is available. In this case the item is not capitalised, but all items are included in the Church's inventory in any case.

Tangible fixed assets for use by charity
These are capitalised if they can be used for more than one year, and cost at least £1,000. They are valued at cost or else, for gifts- in-kind, at a reasonable estimate of their open market value on receipt.

Depreciation is calculated to write off the capitalized cost of fixed assets less their currently anticipated residual fair value over their estimated useful lives as follows:

- Land   Nil
- Fixtures & Fittings   20 years
- Computers   3 years

No depreciation is provided on buildings as the currently estimated residual value of the properties is not less than their carrying value and the remaining useful life of these assets currently exceeds 50 years, so that any depreciation charges would be immaterial.

An impairment review is carried out at each year-end and any resultant loss identified included in expenditure for the year.

Investments
Investments quoted on a recognised stock exchange or whose value derives from them are valued at market value at the year end. Other investment assets are included at PCC's best estimate of market value.

Short term deposits
These are the cash held on deposit either with the CCLA or at the bank.

FUNDS

Unrestricted Funds
These represent the remaining income funds of the PCC that are available for spending on the general purposes of the PCC, including amounts designated by the PCC for fixed assets for its own use or for spending on a future project and which are therefore not included in its 'free reserves' as disclosed in the trustees' report.

Restricted Funds
These are income funds that must be spent on restricted purposes and details of the funds held and restrictions provided are shown in the notes to the accounts.

Endowment Funds
These are restricted funds that must be retained as trust capital either permanently or subject to a discretionary power to spend capital as income, and where the use of any income or other benefit derived from the capital may be restricted or unrestricted. Full details of all their restrictions are shown in the notes to the accounts.

2. INCOME AND ENDOWMENTS

		Unrestricted funds £	Restricted funds £	Endowment funds £	TOTAL 2016 £	TOTAL 2015 £
2(a)	**Voluntary income**					
	Planned giving: Gift Aid donations	107,900	2,600	–	110,500	101,300
	Tax recoverable	24,050	1,500	–	25,550	23,300
	Other	3,900	–	–	3,900	–
	Collections: (open plate)	9,900	1,600	–	11,500	10,600
	Gift days	900	–	–	900	800
	Grants: Major structural renewal	–	162,000	–	162,000	–
	Donations, appeals etc.	1,700	46,800	–	48,500	7,050
	Legacies	11,000	2,250	–	13,250	5,700
		160,400	216,750	–	377,150	148,750
2(b)	**Activities for generating funds**					
	Parish magazine (advertising)	1,100	–	–	1,100	1,050
	Summer fete and Christmas bazaar	2,900	–	–	2,900	2,500
	Fundraising	6,000	–	–	6,000	700
	Rent – temporary let on curate's house	4,200	–	–	4,200	3,700
		14,200	–	–	14,200	7,950
2(c)	**Income from investments**					
	Dividends on CCLA Investment Fund	2,850	1,550	–	4,400	4,000
	Bank and CCLA Deposit Fund Interest	400	950	–	1,350	1,100
		3,250	2,500	–	5,750	5,100
2(d)	**Income from church activities**					
	Fees for weddings and funerals	9,200	–	–	9,200	8,300
	Parish magazine (sales)	2,100	–	–	2,100	1,050
	Church Centre lettings – local community use	4,500	–	–	4,500	3,800
		15,800	–	–	15,800	13,150
	Total income	193,650	219,250	–	412,900	174,950

PAROCHIAL CHURCH COUNCIL OF ST LEDGER'S, AMBRIDGE

NOTES TO THE FINANCIAL STATEMENTS For the year ended 31 December 2016 (continued)

3. EXPENDITURE

	Unrestricted funds £	Restricted funds £	Endowment funds £	TOTAL 2016 £	TOTAL 2015 £
3(a) Church activities					
Missionary and charitable giving					
Overseas: CMS	11,200	–	–	11,200	11,000
South Africa Famine appeal	1,500	1,350	–	2,850	–
Earthquake appeal	–	–	–	–	1,350
Support of Moses Cain and Grace Cross	–	38,650	–	38,650	–
Home: Ambridge Pensioners' Club	3,500	–	–	3,500	3,000
	16,200	40,000	–	56,200	15,350
Ministry: diocesan parish share	91,500	–	–	91,500	87,050
Other ministry costs	9,000	–	–	9,000	8,800
Church running and maintenance	15,750	10,250	–	26,000	25,225
Major repairs – structural renewal	–	189,000	–	189,000	–
Depreciation on curate's house and church equipment	3,000	–	–	3,000	3,000
Sunday school leader training	2,000	–	–	2,000	2,000
Parish magazine costs	2,200	–	–	2,200	1,800
Churchyard upkeep	5,750	–	–	5,750	5,000
Church hall running costs	8,300	5,000	–	13,300	12,525
Printing and stationery	1,500	25	–	1,525	1,200
Bank charges	50	–	–	50	–
	154,300	244,275	–	398,575	161,275
3(b) Raising funds					
Stewardship costs	500	–	–	500	500
Costs of appeals	–	1,250	–	1,250	–
Coffee morning costs	50	–	–	50	–
	550	1,250	–	1,800	500
TOTAL RESOURCES EXPENDED	155,800	245,525	–	401,325	162,450

PAROCHIAL CHURCH COUNCIL OF ST LEDGER'S, AMBRIDGE

NOTES TO THE FINANCIAL STATEMENTS For the year ended 31 December 2016 (continued)

INCOME AND ENDOWMENTS

4   ANALYSIS OF EXPENDITURE INCLUDING ALLOCATION OF SUPPORT COSTS

	Direct costs £	Support costs £	TOTAL £
Church building and maintenance	14,800	950	15,750

	2016 £	2015 £
PCC members induction training	450	200
Independent examiner's remuneration*	500	475
	950	675

* (fees payable to the PCC's examiner for the examination of the financial statements)

5   STAFF COSTS

	2016	2015
Wages and salaries	£4,000	£3,750
Average no. of employees	3	3

During the year the PCC employed an organist, gardener and church cleaner (all part-time) but no payments were large enough to attract social security costs.

There were no employee benefits to key management personnel in the previous or current years.

5(a)   RELATED PARTIES

As the parish organist, Miss M. Joshua, who is a member of the PCC, was paid £1,000 during the year. A small immaterial portion of the expenses paid to the incumbent may have related to his services as chairman of the PCC.

No other payments or expenses were paid to any other PCC member, persons closely connected to them or related parties.

Donations from related parties (PCC members) included £7,250 restored to the major structural renewal project.

PAROCHIAL CHURCH COUNCIL OF ST LEDGER'S, AMBRIDGE

NOTES TO THE FINANCIAL STATEMENTS For the year ended 31 December 2016 (continued)

6. ANALYSIS OF TRANSFER BETWEEN FUNDS

	Unrestricted £	Restricted £	Total £
Major structural renewal	(19,000)	19,000	–

The major structural renewal appeal was started in January 2016 and completed in October 2016. The income received from grants, fundraising and appeal totalled £170,000. The expenditure was £189,000 resulting in a deficit on the restricted project of £19,000. The PCC had anticipated the need for the major repair and had designated £10,000 from general income in the previous year. The PCC approved a transfer of £19,000 from general funds to fund the deficit on the project.

7. FIXED ASSETS

7(a)	**Tangible**	(all unrestricted)		
		Curate's house (freehold) £	Church equipment £	Total £
Cost of valuation	At 1 January 2016	65,000	8,000	73,000
	Disposal	–	(3,000)	(3,000)
	Additions at cost	–	2,000	2,000
	At 31 December 2016	65,000	7,000	72,000
Depreciation	At 1 January 2016	34,000	2,000	36,000
	Withdrawn on disposals	–	(1,000)	(1,000)
	Charge for the year	1,000	2,000	3,000
	At 31 December 2016	35,000	3,000	38,000
Net book value	At 31 December 2016	**30,000**	**4,000**	**34,000**
	At 31 December 2015	31,000	6,000	37,000

The curates house is shown at cost (£65,000), which is the deemed cost under FRS 15 transitional provisions, under which the property's 1994 valuation has not been updated.

Church equipment comprises office equipment. A photocopier was sold during the year for £2,000; its written-down value was £2,000. It was replaced by a smaller machine, cheaper to run.

PAROCHIAL CHURCH COUNCIL OF ST LEDGER'S, AMBRIDGE

NOTES TO THE FINANCIAL STATEMENTS For the year ended 31 December 2016 (continued)

7(b)	Investments	£
	Market value at 1 January 2016	14,500
	Disposal	(9,170)
	Purchases at cost	2,000
	Net gains	6,295
	Market value at 31 December 2016	**13,625**

At the beginning of the year, the ABC stock was sold and produced a gain of £5,855. During the year new investments have been made at various times in the CCLA Church of England Investment Fund. The holding at 31 December 2016 was 3,359 shares, which cost £22,105. The market value at 31 December 2016 represents investments for:

Unrestricted funds	3,355
Restricted funds	7,775
Endowment funds	2,495
	13,625

8. CURRENT ASSETS

8(a)	Investments	£
	Market value at 1 January 2016	15,000
	Purchases at cost	8,605
	Revaluation gain	455
	Market value at 31 December 2016	**24,060**

		2016	2015
		£	£
8(b)	**Debtors (Unrestricted funds)**		
	Tax recoverable	6,240	3,650
	Prepayments and accrued interest	2,075	200
	Other debtors	1,360	150
		9,675	**4,000**

9.	**LIABILITIES**	2016	2015
		£	£
	Amounts falling due in one year (Unrestricted funds)		
	Accruals for utility and other costs	1,000	1,500
	Other creditors	1,700	1,950
	Parish share	–	1,000
		2,700	**4,450**
	Amounts falling due in one year (Unrestricted funds)	500	1,000
	Accruals for utility and other costs	500	1,000

PAROCHIAL CHURCH COUNCIL OF ST LEDGER'S, AMBRIDGE

NOTES TO THE FINANCIAL STATEMENTS For the year ended 31 December 2016 (continued)

10. FUNDS

The restricted funds comprise the church hall fund and the mission fund. The latter represents funds raised for and grants received for the support of the mission work of Moses Cain and Grace Cross, members of the congregation working in the Far East.

The endowment fund is the Jericho bequest, which requires income to be spent on the running of the church hall.

In line with the PCC's policy, a £10,000 provision from the general income has been held in designated funds to part-fund the major structural renewal project. The provision was transferred to restricted funds during 2016 upon completion of the project. At the end of 2016 the designated funds were nil.

11. SUMMARY OF FUND MOVEMENTS

	Unrestricted general structural renewal £	Restricted Church hall £	Restricted Mission £	Restricted Church £	Endowment Church hall	Total
Balance at 1 January 2016	58,935	12,975	1,025	–	2,250	75,185
Incoming resources	193,650	11,325	37,925	170,000	–	412,900
Resources expended	(155,800)	(16,525)	(40,000)	(189,000)	–	(401,325)
Investment gains	5,455	–	1,050	–	245	6,750
Transfer between funds	(19,000)	–	–	19,000	–	–
Balance at 31 December 2016	83,240	7,775	–	–	2,495	93,510

12. SUMMARY OF ASSETS BY FUND

	Unrestricted funds £	Restricted funds £	Endowment funds £	TOTAL 2016 £
Tangible fixed assets	34,000	–	–	34,000
Investment fixed assets	3,355	7,775	2,495	13,625
Current assets	49,085	–	–	49,085
Liabilities				
Amounts falling due in one year	(2,700)	–	–	(2,700)
Amounts falling due after one year	(500)	–	–	(500)
	83,240	7,775	2,495	93,510

13. PRIOR PERIOD COMPARITIVE SOFA RESTATED FOLLOWING TRANSITION TO FRS 102

STATEMENT OF FINANCIAL ACTIVITIES

For the year ending 31 December 2015

	Unrestricted funds £	Restricted funds £	Endowment funds £	TOTAL 2015 £
INCOME AND ENDOWMENTS				
Voluntary income	117,255	31,495	–	148,750
Activities for generating funds	4,250	–	–	4,250
Income from investments	6,750	2,050	–	8,800
Church activities	13,150	–	–	13,150
TOTAL INCOME	141,405	33,545	–	174,950
EXPENDITURE				
Church activities	129,755	32,195	–	161,950
Raising funds	350	150	–	500
TOTAL EXPENDITURE	130,105	32,345	–	162,450
NET INCOME/(EXPENDITURE) BEFORE INVESTMENT GAINS	11,300	1,200	–	12,500
NET GAINS ON INVESTMENTS	70	210	220	500
NET INCOME/(EXPENDITURE)	11,370	1,410	220	13,000
TRANSFER BETWEEN FUNDS	–	–	–	–
NET MOVEMENT IN FUNDS	11,370	1,410	220	13,000
Total funds brought forward	47,565	12,590	2,030	62,185
Total funds carried forward	58,935	14,000	2,250	75,185

chapter 9

Moving between Receipts and Payments and Accruals Accounting

9.1 Introduction

The income threshold at which accruals-based accounting becomes compulsory was raised from £100,000 to £250,000 in 2009 and confirmed in the Charities Act 2011. Although this is far above the gross income level for the vast majority of PCCs, there are some good reasons why a PCC might consider making the move, and this appendix sets out to demystify the accruals basis of annual accounting and explain, in simple terms, what is necessary to make the change.

If moving back from the accruals basis to the simpler and easier Receipts and Payments basis, as a matter of voluntary best practice this chapter explains what could usefully be included in the year of change as helpful extra information for accounts users.

9.2 Background

Over the past few decades a whole raft of accounting legislation has been issued with the objective of removing ambiguities and providing confidence in financial statements. Most recently this has taken on an international aspect as the global nature of organisations and businesses has increased. FRS 102 requires, among other things, the production of a balance sheet and profit and loss account for each financial year. The balance sheet must reflect a 'true and fair view' of the value of the entity at a particular date, and the profit and loss account shows the income and expenditure of the financial year, together with the net resultant net (profit/loss) for the financial year. The accounting requirements for charities that have to follow SORP (FRS 102) for 2016 onwards are no less rigorous. Only where the PCC's annual gross income does not exceed £250,000 is there a statutory opt-out: annual financial reporting is allowed on a simple Receipts and Payments basis as an unregulated 'easy option' in the public interest.

To be sure of a 'true and fair view' there are strict rules in FRS 102 relating to the recognition of assets and liabilities, income and expenditure, which are defined in those rules as rights or obligations to the actual or 'probable' transfer of 'economic benefit'. In practical terms this means that if, for example, the right to some income arises within the financial period and it looks more likely than not that the PCC will benefit in due course and the amount can be reliably quantified, then it must be included as a debtor in the assets section of the balance sheet in so far as the cash has not yet been received by the year end. This is all subtly different from the old 'matching principle' that some readers may be familiar with, whereby revenues were to be matched to the costs that related to them or were incurred in generating them. A further guiding principle is that the accounts are normally prepared on the assumption that the PCC is a 'going concern' for the foreseeable future, and this is then reflected in the basis of valuation of assets (no forced disposals at 'knock-down' prices) and the assessment of likely liabilities (no contract-severance costs to be accrued).

As many PCCs face a challenging financial position, the need for their annual accounts to reflect the diligent and effective management of resources becomes increasingly important and accruals-based annual accounting enables the reader to see this more clearly. The inclusion of the change in the value of any investment assets is significant, as frequently PCCs are having to cash in some of these in order to pay their bills.

9.3 Application of the rules for assets and liabilities

In recognising assets as incoming resources and liabilities as resources expended, accounts-preparation adjustments need to be made to cash-accounting records. These adjustments are in respect of any amounts received or paid that relate to an event occurring in a different year. The two main areas in which this occurs are:

- Any expenses that have been incurred but which have not yet been paid need to be shown as a liability (creditor/accrual) in the balance sheet, the other side of the entry being the expense for the period, thus indicating the true cost for the period. Examples of this might be a utility bill for December or the cost of tuning the organ just before Christmas, which is paid in January; £6,200 for organ tuning in this example.

- Conversely, where an expense such as insurance has been paid in advance, the cost for the year is reduced by the amount relating to the next year, and is balanced with a 'prepayment' asset in the balance sheet.

- Similarly, the right to a Gift Aid tax repayment may exist at the year end and will need to be shown as an asset (debtor) in the balance sheet and included in the income of the current year, although it is not actually received until the next year; £2,240 in this example.

- A further adjustment should be made if significant amounts of wedding fee deposits have been received for next year's weddings; such amounts should be deducted from the fee income for the year and the amount of income received in advance shown as a liability.

- When a significant asset such as a photocopier, which will bring benefits to the parish over several years, is purchased, it should be recognised as an asset and then its cost expensed in the accounts over its anticipated useful life by an accounting process termed depreciation. The accounting policies in the notes to the accounts must state on what basis large items are capitalised and depreciated.

9.4 Reports and terminology

Under Receipts and Payments (R&P) accounting each fund is effectively a summarised cashbook showing the 'ins and outs' of the fund, the excess of receipts over payments (or vice versa!), any transfers between differently restricted funds and the opening and closing cash/bank balances on each of those funds in each case. A PCC with several types of fund can either include them all in a columnar R&P account for the whole PCC or else prepare a separate R&P account for each fund.

The PCC's Statement of Assets and Liabilities then lists all those closing cash/bank balances of all the funds (identifying each fund separately). Money shown as cash at bank must be agreed with the relevant bank statement for each fund by preparing a 'bank reconciliation' document (this does not h ave to be published) showing how the year-end cash book figure has to be adjusted for timing differences arising from items such as cheques written at the end of the month and not yet appearing on the bank statement.

Any money owing to the PCC as at the year end, such as a Gift Aid claim, must also be listed in the statement. This can be done in summary for different kinds if the items are numerous, but separately for each fund. Similarly, any money owed by the PCC as at the year end (liabilities), such as an outstanding bill for the cost of the pre-Christmas organ tuning, must be listed for each fund.

Also listed (descriptively, in order to identify them and also the fund to which they belong) must be any other assets such as investments and property. As 'non-monetary' assets, although listed, these do not have to be included at monetary value.

Even if a cost or value is ascribed to them the amount is not to be added in with the cash, bank and debtors figures for the fund they belong to, though that fund must be identified in each case. This is because the Statement of Assets and Liabilities is not intended as a 'balance sheet', but is just a simple listing, fund by fund, of all monies held by the PCC, all monies owed to it and all monies owed by it, and identifies any significant assets other than those monies.

In a set of accruals-based accounts, however, a balance sheet must be produced that adds in the monetary values of all the non-cash assets and liabilities to enable the resultant fund balances to give a more complete reflection of the true financial position of the PCC. You will see in the following comparison that there are two possible formats that can be used; the more detail that is included in the balance sheet, the less needs to be shown in the notes to the accounts.

A comparison of the two reporting structures and associated terminology follows:

Receipts and Payments Accounts	=	Statement of Financial Activities
Receipts into each fund		Income and endowments
Payments made out of each fund		Expenditure
N/A		Net operating income (net income and endowments before investment gains and losses)
Transfers between different funds of the PCC		Transfers between funds
N/A		Gains/(losses) on any revaluations of functional fixed assets; other recognised gains/losses; any 'extraordinary items' Excess of receipts over payments for that fund
N/A		Net movement in funds
Opening cash at bank and in hand		Fund balances b/fwd 1 January
Closing cash at bank and in hand		Fund balances c/fwd 31 December
Statement of Assets and Liabilities fund by fund	=	**Balance Sheet**
Non-monetary assets retained for ongoing use by the PCC (identifying particulars only)		Fixed assets – Tangible (for own use)
Investment assets (term deposits: amount and term; properties and securities: identifying particulars only)		Investments (securities, term deposits and any other assets (e.g. property) held for investment purposes; social investments)
Monetary assets other than cash/bank amounts, e.g. tax recoverable and other amounts owed to the PCC		Current assets – Stock e.g. books for sale – Debtors e.g. tax recoverable
Deposit account		Short-term deposits
Bank current account		Cash at bank and in hand
Liabilities		Liabilities – Creditors due less than one year – Creditors due more than one year
N/A		Parish Funds that equal the sum of all the assets less the liabilities

9.5   Making the change

A good starting point is to look thoroughly through the simple example of the Receipts and Payments accounts for St Emillion's Church in section 9.9 below and then at the accounts presented in the accrual format. See how the balance sheet matches both assets and liabilities to the total fund balances and see also how further details are included in the notes to accruals-based accounts.

9.6   The opening balance sheet

To produce the opening balance sheet on the accruals basis you will need to look at the previous year's Statement of Assets and Liabilities and add the amounts* of other assets and liabilities into the calculated fund balances.

In this example: £

Property with a cost value of	£59,000
+ Investments with value of	£19,500
+ Cash funds of	£21,000
= Total fund balances	£99,500 at the start of the year

(*This will be cost-based except for any investment securities/properties, for which the year-end market value (estimated if need be) is required under the Regulations.)

On moving back from accruals accounting to the Receipts and Payments basis, the £21,000 will be listed as a monetary asset at the year end, and will also appear in the Receipts and Payments account as the closing balance. And the only identifying particulars for the property and the investment securities will need to appear in the list of assets instead of the above balance sheet values of £59,000 and £19,500.

Note that either the balance sheet or the accounts notes must show how the comparative year values are split across the different categories of funds. It is still necessary to determine this allocation in order to calculate the opening balance on each fund in any case.

In the example, note 4 of the R&P accounts indicates that of the £22,350 of short-term bank deposits, £17,050 belongs to the restricted church fabric fund, while the designated organ fund forms part of the unrestricted funds.

9.7   The Statement of Financial Activities (SOFA)

When changing the method of accounting, both the current and comparative year's figures must be calculated on the same basis. For this reason it is necessary to examine the Statement of Assets and Liabilities for the current and two preceding years and, where necessary, adjust the R&P figures to create the SOFA and its comparatives.

In the reverse direction, changing from accruals to R&P accounting, comparative figures are only optional in the R&P account(s) and Statement of Assets and Liabilities. Nevertheless, as a matter of voluntary best practice, it can be helpful for accounts users to be able to see a note of last year's accrual-figure (i.e. debtor or creditor), if any, that is now included within each of the receipts and payments figures for this year. This can quite easily be shown as a bracketed inset note against each item within the Receipts and Payments Account – e.g. '(includes £2,240 Gift Aid owing from last year)' against 'Gift Aid claims', or '(includes £6,200 owing from last year)' against 'Organ Inspection Cost', for example by reference to the figures in the illustration below.'

In this example there are no 'other monetary assets' or 'liabilities' for the comparative or preceding year but if this were not the case then you would have to look back to those previous years' accounts in order to adjust the prior year figures.

The adjustments to be made in each case for the current year are:

To convert receipts to incoming resources
Take the R&P receipt amount LESS opening debtor PLUS closing debtor
E.g. Gift aid recoverable of £8,700 – zero + £2,240 = £10,940;

To convert expenses to resources expended

Take the R&P expense amount LESS opening liabilities PLUS closing liabilities E.g. Organ inspection costs of zero – zero + £6,200 = £6,200 which forms part of Church activity expenses where £64,050 – zero + £6,200 = £70,250.

The example also shows where the change in the market value of the investment assets needs to be included in the calculation of the final fund balance and detailed in note 5.

9.8 Accounting Policies

The policies adopted must be noted in the case of accruals-based accounts. Refer to the examples for both St Emillion (see below) and St Ledger's (see Chapter 8) for guidance on what should be included.

Note that it is important that the change in accounting basis is highlighted, both in the accounting policies section and in the financial review within the Annual Report.

9.9 Examples to assist in moving between Receipts and Payments accounts and Accrual accounts

RECEIPTS AND PAYMENTS ACCOUNTS

PAROCHIAL CHURCH COUNCIL OF ST EMILLION'S CHURCH, BARCHESTER

FINANCIAL STATEMENTS For the year ended 31 December 2016

Receipts and Payments Accounts

	Note	Unrestricted funds	Restricted funds	Endowment funds	Total funds 2016	Total funds 2015
		£	£	£	£	£
RECEIPTS						
Voluntary receipts:						
Planned giving		29,400	–	–	29,400	27,200
Collections at services		9,900	–	-	9,900	10,600
All other giving/voluntary receipts	5a	2,700	5,800	–	8,500	7,050
Gift Aid recovered		8,700	–	–	8,700	8,300
		50,700	5,800	–	56,500	53,150
Activities for generating funds	5b	3,500	–	–	3,500	4,250
Investment income	5c	4,600	950	–	5,550	5,300
Church activities	5d	5,400	–	–	5,400	5,150
Total receipts		64,200	6,750	–	70,950	67,850
PAYMENTS						
Church activities:						
Diocesan parish contribution		41,500	–	–	41,500	37,050
Clergy and staffing costs		1,900	–	–	1,900	1,800
Church running expenses	5e	13,700	1,850	–	15,550	15,250
Hall running costs		1,200	–	–	1,200	1,200
Mission giving and donations	5f	2,550	1,350	–	3,900	2,550
		60,850	3,200	–	64,050	57,850
Cost of generating funds		500	–	–	500	500
Total payments		61,350	3,200	–	64,550	58,350
Excess of receipts over payments		2,850	3,550	–	6,400	9,500
Transfers between funds	4	(100)	100	–	–	–
		2,750	3,650	–	6,400	9,500
Cash at bank and in hand at 1 Jan		7,600	13,400	–	21,000	11,500
Cash at bank and in hand at 31 Dec		10,350	17,050	–	27,400	21,000

Statement of Assets and Liabilities

	Note	Unrestricted funds	Restricted funds	Endowment funds	TOTAL funds 2016	TOTAL funds 2015
		£	£	£	£	£
Cash Funds						
Bank current account		300	–	–	300	350
Deposit Funds		10,050	17,050		27,100	20,650
		10,350	17,050	–	27,400	21,000
Other monetary assets						
Gift Aid recoverable		2,240	–	–	2,240	–
Investment assets						
Investment fund shares at market value	3	–	–	20,000	20,000	19,500
Assets retained for church use	2	59,000	–	–	59,000	59,000
Liabilities						
Organ cleaning/tune		6,200	–	–	6,200	–

Notes

1. The financial statements of the PCC have been prepared in accordance with the Church Accounting Regulations 2006 using the Receipts and Payments basis

2. Fixed assets retained for church use is the freehold house at 36 Church Street, purchased 5 November 1984, at cost.

3. The Endowment fund, a donation in 1999 by R.H.Smith, has to be retained as a capital fund, but the income is for ordinary church purposes. It is invested in CCLA Church of England Investment fund shares.

4. The movements in designated and restricted funds during the year were:

	Bal b/fwd	Receipts	Payments	Transfer	Bal c/fwd
Designated					
Organ fund	3,300	–	–	2,000	5,300
Restricted					
Church fabric (inc. tower)	13,400	5,050	1,400	–	17,050
Southern Africa Famine appeal	–	1,350	1,350	–	–
Flower fund	–	350	450	100	–
	13,400	6,750	3,200	100	17,050

The transfer to the Organ fund was from ordinary unrestricted funds to meet the balance of the cleaning/tuning costs.

The Fabric fund represents accumulated donations and appeals for fabric maintenance, which can only be spent for that purpose.

The Southern Africa Famine appeal represents funds raised by the Mission and Evangelism Committee to relieve poverty and hardship in the recent famine in Southern Africa.

The Flower fund represents a donation from a parishioner to be spent on Easter lilies in memory of her recently deceased mother.

The cost of the flowers is included in costs of services. A further £100 was designated from the general fund to meet the full cost of lilies.

10. Further Analysis of Receipts and Payments

		Note	Unrestricted funds	Restricted funds	Endowment funds	TOTAL funds 2016	TOTAL funds 2015
			£	£	£	£	£
Receipts							
a)	**All other giving/voluntary receipts**						
	Donations		1,700	5,800	–	7,500	7,050
	Legacy		1,000	–	–	1,000	–
			2,700	5,800	–	8,500	7,050
b)	**Activities for generating funds:**						
	Parish magazine – advertising		1,100	–	–	1,100	1,050
	Summer fete and Christmas bazaar		2,400	–	–	2,400	2,500
	Rummage sales		–	–	–	–	700
			3,500	–	–	3,500	4,250
c)	**Investment income:**						
	Dividends on CCLA Investment Funds		500	–	–	500	500
	Bank and CCLA Deposit Fund interest		400	950	–	1,350	1,100
	Rent – temporary let on curate's house		3,700	–	–	3,700	–
			4,600	950	–	5,550	5,300
d)	**Church activities:**						
	Fees for weddings and funerals		400	–	–	400	300
	Parish magazine income – sales		1,100	–	–	1,100	1,050
	Church Centre lettings – local community use		3,900	–	–	3,900	3,800
			5,400	–	–	5,400	5,150
Payments							
e)	**Church running expenses:**						
	Sunday school teacher training		1,000	–	–	1,000	–
	Organ inspection		–	–	–	–	150
	Costs of services		2,600	450	–	3,050	2,100
	Printing and stationery		1,100	–	–	1,100	1,200
	Church building running expenses		4,700	–	–	4,700	4,800
	Parish magazine printing		1,800	–	–	1,800	1,800
	Church repairs and maintenance		2,500	1,400	–	3,900	5,200
			13,700	1,850	–	15,550	15,250
f)	**Mission giving and donations**						
	CMS		1,200	–	–	1,200	1,200
	Southern Africa Famine appeal		1,350	1,350	–	2,700	–
	Earthquake appeal		–	–	–	–	1,350
			2,550	1,350	–	3,900	2,550

Accrual accounts

PAROCHIAL CHURCH COUNCIL OF ST EMILLION'S CHURCH, BARCHESTER

Financial Statements for the Year Ended 31 December 2016

Statement of Financial Activities

	Note	Unrestricted funds	Restricted funds	Endowment funds	TOTAL 2016	TOTAL 2015
		£	£	£	£	£
Incoming resources						
Voluntary income	2(a)	52,940	5,800	–	58,740	53,150
Activities for generating funds	2(b)	3,500	–	–	3,500	4,250
Investment income	2(c)	4,600	950	–	5,550	5,300
Church activities	2(d)	5,400	–	–	5,400	5,150
Total incoming resources		66,440	6,750	–	73,190	67,850
Resources expended						
Church activities	3(a)	67,050	3,200	–	70,250	57,850
Costs of generating funds		500	–	–	500	500
Total resources expended		67,550	3,200	–	70,750	58,350
Net incoming resources before transfers		(1,110)	3,550	–	2,440	9,500
Transfers between funds	4	(100)	100	–	–	–
Net incoming resources before other recognised gains/(losses)		(1,210)	3,650	–	2,440	9,500
Revaluation gains on investments	4	–	–	500	500	–
Net movement in funds		(1,210)	3,650	500	2,940	9,500
Balances b/fwd 1 January		66,600	13,400	19,500	99,500	90,000
Balances c/fwd 31 December	9	65,390	17,050	20,000	102,440	99,500

Balance Sheet at 31 December 2016

	Note	Unrestricted funds £	Restricted funds £	Endowment funds £	TOTAL 2016 £	TOTAL 2015 £
Fixed assets						
Tangible	6	59,000	–	–	59,000	59,000
Investments	4	–	–	20,000	20,000	19,500
		59,000	–	20,000	79,000	78,500
Current assets						
Debtors	7	2,240	–	–	2,240	–
Short-term deposits		10,050	17,050	–	27,100	20,650
Cash at bank and in hand		300	–	–	300	350
		12,590	17,050	–	29,640	21,000
Current liabilities						
Creditors	8	6,200	–	–	6,200	–
Net current assets		6,390	17,050	–	23,440	21,000
Total net assets	9	65,390	17,050	20,000	102,440	99,500

			2016		2015
Represented by parish funds					
Unrestricted			65,390		66,600
Restricted			17,050		13,400
Endowment			20,000		19,500
	9		102,440		99,500

107

Notes

1.   Accounting policies

Basis of financial statements

The financial statements have been prepared under the Church Accounting Regulations 2006 in accordance with applicable accounting standards and the current Statement of Recommended Practice, Accounting and Reporting by Charities and applicable accounting standard FRS 102.

The financial statements have been prepared under the historical cost convention except for investment assets, which are shown at market value. The financial statements include all transactions, assets and liabilities for which the PCC is responsible in law. They do not include the accounts of church groups that owe their main affiliation to another body, nor those that are informal gatherings of church members.

This is the first year that the accounts have been prepared using the accruals accounting method and this has resulted in the significant year-on-year variation in the Gift Aid recovered income and organ inspection costs.

Fund accounting

Endowment funds are funds, the capital of which must be retained either permanently or at the PCC's discretion; the income derived from the endowment is to be used either as restricted or unrestricted income funds depending upon the purpose for which the endowment was established in the first place.

Restricted funds comprise (a) income from endowments that is to be expended only on the restricted purposes intended by the donor, and (b) revenue donations or grants for a specific PCC activity intended by the donor. Where these funds have unspent balances, interest on their pooled investment is apportioned to the individual funds on an average balance basis.

Unrestricted funds are income funds that are to be spent on the PCC's general purposes.

Designated funds are general funds set aside by the PCC for use in the future. Project funds are designated for particular projects for administration purposes only. Funds designated as invested in fixed assets for the PCC's own use are abated in line with those assets' annual depreciation charges in the SOFA. Designated funds remain unrestricted and the PCC will move any surplus to other general funds.

Incoming resources

Planned giving, collections and similar donations are recognised when received. Tax refunds are recognised when the incoming resource to which they relate is received. Grants and legacies are accounted for when the PCC is entitled to the use of the resources, their ultimate receipt is considered reasonably certain and the amounts due are readily quantifiable. Dividends are accounted for when declared receivable, interest as and when accrued by the payer. All incoming resources are accounted for gross.

Resources expended

Grants and donations are accounted for when paid over, or when awarded, if that award creates a binding or constructive obligation on the PCC. The diocesan parish share expected to be paid over is accounted for when due. All other expenditure is generally recognised when it is incurred and is accounted for gross.

Fixed assets

Consecrated and benefice property is not included in the accounts in accordance with s.10(2)(a) and (c) of the Charities Act 2011.

Movable church furnishings held by the vicar and churchwardens on special trust for the PCC and which require a faculty for disposal are inalienable property, listed in the church's inventory, which can be inspected (at any reasonable time). For anything acquired prior to 2000 there is insufficient cost information available and therefore such assets are not valued in the financial statements. Subsequently no individual item has cost more than £1,000 so all such expenditure has been written off when incurred.

No cost information is available for the curate's house so it is included at a deemed cost being its 1994 valuation of £65,000 (including £15,000 estimated freehold land value). The building is being depreciated at £1,000 per annum with effect from 2003 on the basis of its expected useful life of 50 years.

Equipment used within the church premises is depreciated on a straight-line basis over four years. Individual items of equipment with a purchase price of £500 or less are written off when the asset is acquired.

Investments are valued at market value at 31 December.

2. Incoming resources

	Unrestricted funds	Restricted funds	TOTAL 2016	Unrestricted funds	Restricted funds	TOTAL 2015
	£	£	£	£	£	£
a) Voluntary income						
Planned giving	29,400	–	29,400	27,200	–	27,200
Collections at services	9,900	–	9,900	10,600	–	10,600
Sunday donations	1,700	5,800	7,500	2,050	5,000	7,050
Legacy	1,000	–	1,000	–		
Gift Aid recovered	10,940	–	10,940	8,300	–	8,300
	52,940	5,800	58,740	48,150	5,000	53,150
b) Activities for generating funds:						
Parish magazine – advertising	1,100	–	1,100	1,050	–	1,050
Summer fete and Christmas	2,400	–	2,400	2,500	–	2,500
Rummage sales	–	–	–	700		700
	3,500	–	3,500	4,250	–	4,250
c) Investment income:						
Dividends on CCLA Funds	500	–	500	500	–	500
Bank and CCLA Interest	400	950	1,350	1,100	650	1,100
Rent on curate's house	3,700	–	3,700	3,700	–	3,700
	4,600	950	5,550	5,300	650	5,300
d) Church activities:						
Fees for weddings and funerals	400	–	400	300	–	300
Parish magazine income – sales	1,100	–	1,100	1,050	–	1,050
Church Centre lettings	3,900	–	3,900	3,800	–	3,800
	5,400	–	5,400	5,150	–	5,150
Total Income	66,440	6,750	73,190	62,2	5,650	67,850

3. Expenditure

	Unrestricted funds	Restricted funds	TOTAL 2016	Unrestricted funds	Restricted funds	TOTAL 2015
	£	£	£	£	£	£
a) Church activity expenses						
Mission giving and donations						
CMS	1,200	–	1,200	1,200	–	1,200
Southern Africa Famine appeal	1,350	1,350	2,700	–		
Earthquake appeal	–	–	–	1,350	–	1,350
	2,550	1,350	3,900	2,550	–	2,550
Diocesan parish contribution	41,500	–	41,500	37,050	–	37,050
Clergy and staffing costs	1,900	–	1,900	1,800	–	1,800
Sunday school teacher training	1,000	–	1,000	–	–	
Organ inspection	6,200	–	6,200	150	–	150
Costs of services	2,600	450	3,050	2,100	–	2,100
Printing and stationery	1,100	–	1,100	1,200	–	1,200
Church building running expenses	4,700	–	4,700	4,800	–	4,800
Parish magazine printing	1,800	–	1,800	1,800	–	1,800
Church repairs and maintenance	2,500	1,400	3,900	2,000	3,200	5,200
Hall running costs	1,200	–	1,200	1,200	–	1,200
	67,050	3,200	70,250	54,650	3,200	57,850

4. Investments

CCLA Investment:	Market value 01/01/2016	Purchases	Disposals	Revaluation	Market value 31/12/2016	
245.9 shares in a/c 1234S	19,500				500	20,000

5. Transfers between funds

The transfer to the designated organ fund was from ordinary unrestricted funds to meet the balance of the clean/tune costs.

The transfer to the restricted flower fund was from ordinary unrestricted funds to meet the balance of the cost of the Easter lilies.

6. Tangible assets

This comprises the freehold house at 36 Church Street, purchased 5 November 1984, and shown at cost. It is retained for church use.

7. Debtors

Gift Aid recoverable	2,240	–

8. Creditors

Organ cleaning/tune	6,200	–

9. Funds

The movements in designated and restricted funds during the year were:

	Bal b/fwd	Income	Expenditure	Transfers	Market value	Bal c/fwd
	£	£	£	£	£	£
Unrestricted funds						
General	63,300	66,440	67,550	(2,100)	–	60,090
Designated funds						
Organ fund	3,300	–	–	2,000	–	5,300
Restricted funds						
Church fabric (inc. tower)	13,400	5,050	1,400	–	–	17,050
S Africa famine appeal	–	1,350	1,350	–	–	–
Flower fund	–	350	450	100	–	–
Endowment funds						
R. H. Smith fund	19,500	–	–	–	500	20,000
	99,500	73,190	70,750	–	500	102,440

The fabric fund represents accumulated donations and appeals for fabric maintenance, which can only be spent for that purpose.

The Southern Africa Famine appeal represents funds raised by the mission and evangelism committee to relieve poverty and hardship in the recent famine in Southern Africa.

The flower fund represents a donation from a parishioner to be spent on Easter lilies in memory of her recently deceased mother. The cost of the flowers is included in costs of services.

The endowment fund, a donation in 1999 by R. H. Smith, has to be retained as a capital fund, but the income is for ordinary church purposes. It is invested in CCLA Church of England Investment Fund shares.

chapter 10

Group Consolidated Accounts and Annual Reports

For PCCs whose combined gross income (including all subsidiaries) exceeds the Charities Act current audit threshold of £1m for the year, group consolidated accounts and Annual Reports are a statutory requirement.

Thus a PCC having trustee-body control of a connected charity from which it can draw benefit for its mission in the parish, but which it does not have to account for in its own accounts as a PCC, or (more rarely) beneficial control of a non-charitable body such as a wholly or partly owned trading company that it uses to generate additional revenues for the work of the PCC, must consolidate the statutory accounts of all such 'subsidiary undertakings' in group accounts in addition to its own accounts.

Modules 28 and 29 of SORP (FRS 102) paragraphs 407–418, which deal with compliance with FRS 9, also applies to any PCC not exempted from preparing consolidated accounts. FRS 9 requires it to include in its accounts any material interests it may have in any kind (charitable or fundraising) of consortium undertaking (corporate 'joint venture') or 'associated' undertaking (equity/voting interests above 20% but below the 50% of a joint venture, except where there is no significant influence on the investee's management) – as well as for what the SORP calls a 'joint arrangement'. The latter could obviously include any kind of participation in a non-corporate shared activity of a multi-denominational nature, thus not only the commercial kind of profit-sharing partnership activity that many companies engage in.

The SORP explains that the accounting treatment depends on whether the investing charity prepares consolidated accounts (when the 'equity' method of accounting* must be used for 'associated undertakings' and corporate joint ventures), or only its own entity accounts.

(*The equity method of accounting requires the charity's interest in the investee-entity to be 'initially recognised at its cost (the transaction price paid), including any cost incurred making the investment (transaction costs). The initial cost equates to the fair value of net assets acquired, plus any goodwill. For more information on the equity method, refer to section 14 of FRS 102.' – SORP module 28.11.)

In its own entity accounts, however, the charity's interest in the investee-entity 'must be included in the accounts at cost less impairment (the cost model) or, if the fair value of the charity's interest can be measured reliably, the charity may opt to measure its interest at fair value with any gain or loss taken through income and expenditure'. (SORP (FRS 102), module 29.12)

Modules 28 and 29 set out detailed disclosure requirements that include naming each such investee-entity, the accounting policy adopted for it and the carrying amount of its investment in such entities, as well as other information needed for strict compliance with FRS 102.

Parent charities invariably combine their group accounts with their entity accounts in the same publication, as this minimises the paperwork entailed and also allows them to take advantage of the Charity Commission's continuing non-statutory concession to publish their group SOFA without their own (entity) SOFA and instead to report the key figures from the latter as an accounts note.

The group accounts must be accompanied by a group Annual Report, which replaces the usual PCC Annual Report. This group report includes specified disclosures in respect of the activities and performance of the subsidiary undertakings in relation to the PCC, but is otherwise the same as the Annual Report to be prepared by any other auditable PCC.

See group-accounting legislation contained in the 2011 Act and SI 2008/629.

chapter 11

Independent Examination

11.1 Introduction

The flowchart in Chapter 1, paragraph 1.2 sets out the thresholds for the independent examination or audit of PCC annual financial statements.

All PCCs below the audit threshold may choose to have their financial statements independently examined rather than audited. A major donor or grant maker may require the financial statements to be audited even though an independent examination might otherwise have been chosen. An audit is a more onerous form of scrutiny and must be carried out by a registered auditor but an auditor can be asked to act as an examiner. PCCs that can choose independent examination, rather than an audit, are encouraged to do so.

11.2 What does the PCC have to do?

A suitable examiner has to be appointed by the Annual Parochial Church Meeting (APCM). The PCC will have to consider carefully the suitability of a prospective independent examiner in good time in order to guide the meeting in its appointment.

11.3 Can an examiner be paid?

The PCC is entitled to pay a reasonable fee to an independent examiner for their services. If the services of a competent examiner cannot be obtained on a voluntary basis, the PCC should be prepared to pay a modest fee, which is a proper charge on its funds. The PCC should not be pressured into appointing an examiner acting in a voluntary capacity just because they will do the work free of charge. The PCC must be satisfied that the examiner has the requisite ability and experience.

11.4 Who can be an independent examiner?

An independent examiner is described in Section 145 of the Charities Act 2011 as:

'an independent person who is reasonably believed by the trustees to have the requisite ability and practical experience to carry out a competent examination of the financial statements'.

> *The term 'independent examiner' does not exclude an accountant or, indeed, a registered auditor, but recognises that the scrutiny is less onerous than an audit.*

In respect of PCCs with gross income over £250,000, the independent examiner must have a 'recognised' qualification as per Charities Act 2011. Should, however, the PCC's gross assets in the balance sheet exceed £3.26m, an audit is required.

11.5 What does 'independent' mean?

- For an examiner to be independent that individual must have no connection with the PCC that might appear to be prejudicial to an impartial examination of the financial statements.

- The following persons will be considered to have a connection with the PCC that makes it inappropriate for them to be an examiner:

(a)   a member of the PCC or any of its sub-committees (this exclusion is included in the Church Representation Rules);

(b)   an employee of the PCC, or a person receiving benefit or support from PCC funds by way of a gift (other than a fee received as an examiner);

(c)   a child, parent, grandchild, grandparent, brother or sister, spouse, civil partner, business partner or employee of any person who falls within sub-paragraph (a) or (b) above.

An independent examiner can, however, be a member of the Church with their name on the electoral roll.

11.6 What sort of people can be appointed?

● The Church Accounting Regulations require an external scrutiny of the financial statements for all PCCs, even though the Charities Act does not require external scrutiny where gross income is up to and including £25,000.

● For PCCs with gross income that does not exceed £250,000 for the year, and with financial statements prepared on the receipts and payments basis, an appropriate independent examiner would be someone familiar with business and financial matters. For all accruals accounts the examiner also needs to be familiar with Charity accounting and regulation but they need not be a relevant formal qualification.

● PCCs with gross income between £250,000 and £1m for the year and with a balance sheet value of gross assets not exceeding £3.26 million, must appoint an appropriately qualified accountant or examiner (see CC32 on the Charity Commission website: www.charitycommission.gov.uk) to carry out the independent examination.

● PCCs with gross income in excess of £1m for the year, or where gross income is greater than £250,000 for the year and the balance sheet value of gross assets is in excess of £3.26 million, must have an audit by a registered auditor.

● Where group accounts, consolidating the accounts of the PCC and its subsidiaries, have to be prepared, the examiner must also have the requisite knowledge of the statutory group accounting requirements.

11.7 How should an examiner's requisite ability be checked?

Whether an examiner has the requisite ability will depend very much on the size and complexity of the PCC's financial statements as well as on the examiner's individual experience.

● The duty to seek evidence of the ability of a prospective independent examiner rests with the PCC. If the prospective independent examiner is not known to the members of the PCC, the PCC should consider asking to see a CV, taking independent references and possibly forming a small group to interview candidates.

● Difficulties can arise where the examiner has been recommended by an individual member of the PCC, who has then made the only contact with them. There have been cases where it was found that the examiner never existed!

11.8 What is appropriate 'practical experience'?

The PCC should satisfy itself that a prospective examiner has practical experience of preparing or reviewing and evaluating the financial statements of comparable organisations as well as experience of charity regulation and can readily understand the PCC's financial statements and interpretation of matters of 'material significance to the regulator'.

11.9   How does the PCC know what it has to provide to the examiner?

The treasurer should discuss fully with the prospective examiner the work of the PCC and its expectations. Help will be found in the CC32 directions and guidance notes on the duties of an examiner. In some dioceses guidance and advice may be available, or treasurers in neighbouring parishes or deanery finance officers may be in a position to assist. The examiner's duties must be followed to ensure that the requirements of the Church Accounting Regulations 2006 are met. The Charity Commission guidance
on independent examination is in the following publications:

Independent Examination of Charity Accounts: Trustees' Guide (CC31) Independent Examination of Charity Accounts: Examiners' Guide (CC32).

11.10   What happens when the PCC and the APCM appoint an examiner?

Particularly for larger PCCs, it is recommended that, in order to reduce the chance of any misunderstanding, the independent examiner should write to the PCC detailing its accounting responsibilities and the examiner's statutory responsibilities. The content of the letter should be agreed with the PCC and a sample letter is shown below. The same distinction of responsibilities will normally be required by a professional examiner or auditor to be included in the annual report and accounts.

Some examiners of PCCs will probably document the agreed terms of engagement in this way, but the matters set out here should be discussed and agreed with all independent examiners prior to the examination.

The examiner must be given sufficient time in which to complete the examination.

The PCC will need to approve a motion for the appointment of the independent examination at the APCM. A suitable form of words is:

> The PCC has elected to subject the financial statements to independent examination and, therefore, having made appropriate enquiries, propose [insert the name of the examiner] as independent examiner until the next APCM.

Example: This following example which PCCs may wish to use but please be aware that the terms of engagement may vary from time to time according to changes in regulatory requirements and/ obligations of independent examiners.

[Note: The phrases in square brackets should be omitted when the examination is of accounts on the receipts and payments basis.]

St Ledger's Church

Dear members of the PCC,

Engagement as independent examiner

The purpose of this letter is to set out in confirmation of our recent discussions the basis on which I am prepared to act as independent examiner to prepare a report in respect of the PCC's financial statements for the year ended 31 December 2016, and for future years until further notice, in accordance with section 145 of the Charities Act 2011 ('the Act') and the Church Accounting Regulations 2006 ('the Regulations').

Responsibilities of members of the PCC

As members of the PCC, you are responsible for maintaining proper accounting records and for preparing accounts which [give a true and fair view and] have been prepared in accordance with the Regulations.

You are also responsible for determining whether, in respect of the year (and the preceding two years), the PCC meets the conditions for exemption from an audit of the accounts set out in section 144(1) of the Act and the Regulations, and for providing me with information and explanations required for my examination.

Responsibilities of the independent examiner

I shall plan my work on the basis that an independent examiner's report on the accounts is required for the year, unless you inform me in writing to the contrary. As an independent examiner I have a statutory duty to state in my report whether any matter has come to my attention in connection with the examination which gives me reasonable cause to believe that in any material respect:

- accounting records have not been properly kept in accordance with section 130 of the Act; or

- the accounts do not accord with the accounting records or do not comply with the Regulations [other than in respect of the requirement for a true and fair view].

I also have a statutory duty to disclose in my report [inconsistencies between the accounts and the annual report and] matters coming to my attention in connection with the examination to which, in my opinion, attention should be drawn in order to enable a proper understanding of the accounts to be reached.

Should my work lead me to conclude that the PCC is not entitled to exemption from an audit of the accounts or should I be unable to reach a conclusion on this matter, then I will not issue any report and will notify you in writing of the reasons. In these circumstances, if appropriate, I will discuss with you the need to appoint an auditor.

Scope of the independent examiner's work

My work will be carried out in accordance with general directions setting out the duties of an independent examiner issued by the Charity Commission and as contained in the Church guidance.

My work as independent examiner will be a less onerous form of scrutiny than an audit of the accounts in accordance with Auditing Standards. My examination will include a review of the accounting records kept by the PCC and a comparison of the accounts presented with those records. It will also include a review of the accounts and consideration of any unusual items or disclosures identified. In such cases where I identify an unusual item, I will seek explanations from the PCC, and may carry out verification and vouching procedures where I require further clarification. [Similarly I will make assessments of the estimates and judgements made by you in your preparation of the accounts where they are material to the accounts.]

My work cannot be relied on to identify the occasional omission or insignificant error, nor to disclose breaches of trust or statute, neglect or fraud which may have taken place and which it is the responsibility of the PCC to guard against. However, I would be obliged to report direct to regulators any matters of material significance coming to light in the course of my work.

Should I become aware, for any reason, that the accounts may be misleading and we cannot agree approp- riate amendments, and I then conclude that the matter cannot be adequately dealt with in my report, I will not issue any report a nd will withdraw from the engagement, and will notify you in writing of the reasons.

As part of my normal procedures, I may request you to provide written confirmation of any information or explanations given by you orally during the course of my work.

Fees

I am prepared to waive my fee for this examination.

Confirmation

Once it has been agreed, this letter will remain effective until it is replaced or until I cease to hold the position of independent examiner. I shall be grateful if you will kindly confirm your agreement to the terms of this letter by arranging for the signature, and return, of the attached copy, or let me know if the terms of this letter are not in accordance with your understanding of my terms of appointment.

Yours faithfully

11.11 The Charity Commission's statutory Directions

- The Charity Commission's Directions provide the procedural basis or framework to define how the reporting duties of the examiner must be met. The Directions are made by the Charity Commission under powers given in the Charities Act 2011 and set out the areas of work that must be covered in any examination.

- The Charity Commission is aware that volunteer examiners, who are not charging a fee, are giving their time freely for the benefit of the charity sector. In the event of a concern arising about the adequacy of an independent examination carried out by a volunteer, the Commission will take into account the nature of the voluntary role and be proportionate in their approach when considering any failure in the examination process, provided the examiner has acted reasonably and honestly and the PCC has acted with due care.

- Where the examiner is charging a fee or receiving payment it is expected that the services provided will be to a professional standard.

In all cases the examiner:

- must demonstrate appropriate technical knowledge, including familiarity with the Statement of Recommended Practice for Charities (the SORP) and Charity Commission regulatory policy and practice;

- must carry out their work fully in accordance with the Charity Commission's Directions; and

- must be competent by virtue of their ability and experience, to fulfil their statutory duty to report matters of material significance to the Charity Commission.

The actual Directions are contained in the Charity Commission's publication (CC32).

11.12 Audit/Independent examination comparison

Procedure	Audit	Independent examination
Opinion required as to whether financial statements show a true and fair view	Yes	No
Level of assurance given	High, positive	Moderate, negative
Check accounting records to establish entitlement to independent examination instead of audit	n/a	Yes
Obtain understanding of the PCC's organisation, accounting system, activities and nature of its assets, liabilities, incoming resources and application of resources in order to plan appropriate procedures	Yes	Yes
Record the procedures carried out and document matters that are important to support conclusions reached or statements provided in the report	Yes	Yes
Consideration of accounting records (i.e. that they are in accordance with section 130 of the Charities Act 2011)	Yes	Yes
Analytical review	Yes	Yes
Substantive testing, e.g. vouching source documents, physical inspection of fixed assets, obtaining bank confirmation of balances, inspection of investment certificates etc	Yes	No – unless the analytical review shows unusual items for which the PCC cannot give satisfactory explanations
Review financial statements for conformity with applicable rules on form and content	Yes	Yes
Considering conformity with the current charities SORP and the PCC's financial viability. Consider any significant estimate or judgement made in preparing the financial statements.	Yes	Yes (with the exception of true and fair view). Enquiry of the PCC (accruals-based accounts)
Post balance sheet events	Obtain sufficient appropriate evidence	
Identify and report on any major inconsistencies between any financial references in the annual report and financial statements	Yes	Yes
Obtain all information and explanations needed to carry out the scrutiny – report any failure to the PCC and other bodies (as appropriate)	Yes	Yes

Acknowledgements

The support of the following members of the Diocesan Accounts Sub-groups in preparing this guide is gratefully acknowledged:

Ashley Ellis, (Chairperson), Joint Diocesan Secretary, Leeds Diocese

Shaun Birch, Finance Manager, Leeds Diocese

Susan Bunting, Director of Finance, Norwich Diocese

Greyham Dawes, Director – Not-for-profit Unit, Crowe Clark Whitehill LLP

Catherine Evans, Finance Manager, York Diocese

Carol Fletcher, Senior Financial Planner, Finance and Resources, Church Commissioners

Bryan Lewis, Finance Manager, Leeds Diocese

Mary Makin, Diocesan Accountant, Guildford, Portsmouth and Winchester Dioceses

Katy Reade, former Diocesan Accountant, St Edmundsbury & Ipswich Diocese

Sharon Sawyer, Senior Finance Officer, Leeds Diocese

Heather Burge, PA to Ashley Ellis, Joint Diocesan Secretary, Leeds Diocese

Index

Note: Page numbers in italic type indicate tables and examples.